Vegan Flavors of the Caribbean

**Over 100 Recipes to Choose From.
Many are Raw and Gluten-Free.
All are Healthy and Delicious!**

By Latoya Carter

TEACH Services, Inc.
PUBLISHING
www.TEACHServices.com • (800) 367-1844

World rights reserved. This book or any portion thereof may not be copied or reproduced in any form or manner whatever, except as provided by law, without the written permission of the publisher, except by a reviewer who may quote brief passages in a review.

The author assumes full responsibility for the accuracy of all facts and quotations as cited in this book. The opinions expressed in this book are the author's personal views and interpretations, and do not necessarily reflect those of the publisher.

This book is provided with the understanding that the publisher is not engaged in giving spiritual, legal, medical, or other professional advice. If authoritative advice is needed, the reader should seek the counsel of a competent professional.

Copyright © 2018 Latoya Carter

Copyright © 2018 TEACH Services, Inc.

ISBN-13: 978-1-4796-0787-7 (Paperback)

ISBN-13: 978-1-4796-0788-4 (ePub)

ISBN-13: 978-1-4796-0789-1 (Mobi)

Library of Congress Control Number: 2018930918

The website references in this book have been shortened using a URL shortener and redirect service called 1ref.us, which TEACH Services manages. If you find that a reference no longer works, please contact us and let us know which one is not working so that we can correct it. Any personal website addresses that the author included are managed by the author. TEACH Services is not responsible for the accuracy or permanency of any links.

Image Credits:

Latoya Carter; eskay lim/Bigstock.com; Ulianna/Bigstock.com; lzf/Bigstock.com; Irina Burakova/Bigstock.com; oysy/Bigstock.com; cdm-primorsko/Bigstock.com; accept/Bigstock.com; urbanlight/Bigstock.com; Tanya14/Bigstock.com; Milkos/Bigstock.com; bane.m/Bigstock.com; igordutina/Bigstock.com; Dron-M/Bigstock.com; napior/Bigstock.com; Anikona/Bigstock.com; sierpniowka/Bigstock.com; bhofack22/Bigstock.com; Yastremska/Bigstock.com; mcfields/Bigstock.com; Alatielin/Bigstock.com; LiliGraphie/Bigstock.com; nata_vkusidey/Bigstock.com; zoeytoja/Bigstock.com; Anna_Shepulova/Bigstock.com; evgenyb/Bigstock.com; Cabeca de Marmore/Bigstock.com; cegli/Bigstock.com; Beauty Nature/Bigstock.com; Elena Shashkina/Bigstock.com; Sea Wave/Bigstock.com; Brian Lasenby/Bigstock.com; Anna Pustynnikova/Bigstock.com; Jag_cz/Bigstock.com; venakp/Bigstock.com; muslimova/Bigstock.com; Kovaleva Katerina/Bigstock.com; Volff/Bigstock.com; PitchyPix/Bigstock.com; Nick Dale/Bigstock.com; morisfoto/Bigstock.com; ThreeArt/Bigstock.com; ksumano/Bigstock.com; pikepicture/Bigstock.com; anamejia18/Bigstock.com; Ashva/Bigstock.com; Zharkusha/Bigstock.com; esal/Bigstock.com; October22/Bigstock.com; Myroslava/Bigstock.com; Amelie11/Bigstock.com; Thanthip H./Bigstock.com; Anatoly Repin/Bigstock.com; enotmutant/Bigstock.com; oysy/Bigstock.com; wrangel/Bigstock.com; Medusa81/Bigstock.com; Anna Kucherova/Bigstock.com; PaulCowan/Bigstock.com; west1/Bigstock.com; 115206971/Bigstock.com

Table of Contents

    Cooking Steps to Follow 11
    Equivalents 11
    Definitions of Less Common Ingredients 12

Breakfast Foods 15

    Pancakes 16
    Granola 16
    Breakfast Millet 17
    Roti 17
    Scrambled Tofu 18
    Baked Green And Yellow Plantain 18
    Sweeter Baked Yellow Plantains 19
    Hash Browns 19

Breads 21

    Basic Bread Dough 22
    Tennis Rolls 22
    Amadama Bread 23
    Corn Bread 23
    Pinwheels 23
    Coconut Rolls 24
    Gluten Stuffed Bread 24
    Pizza 25
    Unleavened Bread (Communion Bread) 25
    Pine Tarts 25
    Cheese Rolls 26
    Crackers 26
    Sesame Sticks 26
    Flax Millét Crackers 26
    Flaxseed Crescents 27
    Flaxseed Gel 27
    Meh Pot 28
    Proteins 29

Entrees 31

    Macaroni with Vegan Cheese 32
    Baked Katahar or Jack Fruit 32
    Gluten Tofu Loaf 33
    Prepared Gluten 33
    Eggplant Stew 34

Baked Fries. 34
Pigeon Peas Stew 34
Colored Rice 34
Okara Fish Cakes or Fingers 35
Oatmeal Patties 35
Lasagna. 36
Potato Pie 36
Roasted Eggplant Rolls. 36
Curry Katahar or Jackfruit or Potatoes 37
Mashed or Cubed Provision (Ground Vegetables) 37
Burgers 38
Spinach Quiche 38
Meatballs or Burger Patties 38
Meatballs or Burger Patties (continued) 39
Zucchini Cakes. 40
Basil Rice 40
Black-eyed Peas Stew 41
Dahl. 41
Split Peas Balls. 41
Mashed Potatoes 42
Cassava Puffs 42
Cook-up 42
Pak Choi or Bok Choy Stew 43
Channa 43
Ackee 43
Fats 44

Desserts 45

Carob Pudding. 46
Carob No Cook Pudding or Soft Serve 46
Sweet Loaf 46
Orange Cake or Muffins 47
Coconut Ice Cream 47
Ice Cream 48
Coconut Mango Ice Cream. 48
Coconut Buns. 48
Cassava Pone 49
Pumpkin Pone 49
Sugar Cake 49
Guava Cheese 49
Conkie. 50
Fruit Cake. 50
Rice Custard Tarts 51
No Cook Dessert 51
Raisin Oat Cookies 52
Brownies. 52

Pineapple Cheesecake 53
Carob Fudge Topping 53
Key Lime Pie 54
Raw Carrot Cake 54
Frosting Cream 54
Peanut Butter Cookies 55
Mom's Cookies 55
No Bake Cookies 55
Carob No Chocolate Bars 56
"Reece's"-like Fudge 56
Candied Pecans 56
Fudgesicles 57
Fudge 57
Caramel Popcorn 57

Butters, Creams, Dressings, Etc. 59

Butter 60
Date Butter. 60
Dipping Sauce 60
Pizza Sauce 60
Spaghetti Sauce 61
Spicy Sweet and Sour Sauce 61
White Cheese 61
Yellow Sweet Pepper Cheese Sauce. 62
Garbanzo Spread. 62
Olive Spread. 62
Cucumber Relish 63
Green Mango Sour 63
Cucumber Sour 63
Homemade Ketchup 63
Salsa 64
Batter 64
Eggless Mayonnaise. 64
Sunflower Seed Dressing 65
Salad Dressing 65
Sesame Seed Dressing. 65
Cucumber Dressing 65
Oil-free Dressing 66
Seasoned Bread Crumbs 66
Curry Powder 66
Boulange or Eggplant Choka 67
Coconut Choka 67
Tamarind Chutney 67
Almond Milk 68
Soy Milk and Soybean Cheese 68

Soups and Salads...69

    5 Bean Salad.. 70
    Bulgur Taco Salad 70
    Pasta Salad 70
    Cucumber Avocado Salad............................... 71
    Cabbage Quinoa Salad 71
    Normal Salad 71
    Black Olive Salad... 71
    Black-eyed Pea Salad..................................... 71
    Simple Tomato Soup 72
    Guyanese Soup 72
    Broccoli Cheese Soup 72

Juices and Shakes..73

    Green Drink Recipe 74
    Papaya Punch 74
    Carob No Chocolate Milkshake...................... 74
    Watermelon Pineapple Juice 74
    Cane Juice 75
    Sour Sop Smoothie 75

Kitchen Pharmacy..77

About the Author...78

Index..79

Preface

*"This cookbook is great for mothers and children,
as well as husbands and wives.
Cooking is a family affair in the Caribbean."*

Mother, Mother

"Mother, mother see what I've done!"

A mess of rubbish piled high on the ground.

She looks at him with a sympathizing frown,

"You shouldn't have done this, but I love you anyhow."

"Mother, mother look at this!"

Arrests her attention as she makes the cakes.

Chubby hands in the flour on the kitchen tile,

With great patience she responds with a kind smile,

"You'll be a great chef, but in a little while."

A Conversation

"Honey what would you like to eat?"

"F-O-O-D," he spells as he takes a seat.

"You rarely tell me what kind," she mutters underneath her breath.

"Anything," he tells her, "that will prevent starving to death."

"And when I go on camp, what will you do?"

"Well dear, the cookbook of course will then replace you."

"Nothing can replace me," she quickly replies.

"Yes, I agree" he counters with a twinkle in his eyes.

Nutrition is the study of the interactions that occur between living things and nutrients (food).

<u>Rules:</u> The first rule of nutrition is to be sure to include a variety of foods in the diet during the year. While variety is essential over time, the second rule of nutrition is that individual meals should be kept simple. The third rule of good nutrition requires that within each individual meal we eat a good supply of fruits and vegetables, of whole grains and of nuts and seeds.

You are in the right book!

It's all about COOKING and FOOD!

<u>Proteins:</u> Pandas, elephants, giraffes, cows, horses? What do these have to do with a cookbook? Rest assured they aren't in any of the recipes, but more than this: what do these animals all have in common? Well, they are all strong, some are very big, some are slow, and some are quick. If we would pay attention to nature, we could learn many lessons. If you notice many of these animals have much more muscle than we do, and they have no protein deficiency on a plant based diet! That's the commonality—they are all herbivores. But more inside on proteins. *Now, let's cook!*

Great Quotes

*"The doctor of the future will no longer treat the human frame with drugs,
but rather will cure and prevent disease with NUTRITION"
(Thomas Edison).*

*"When diet is wrong, medicine is of no use. When diet is correct, medicine is of no need."
(Ayurvedic Proverb).*

*"If you don't take care of your body, where are you going to live?"
(Unknown).*

*"Sickness comes on horseback but departs on foot"
(Dutch Proverb).*

*Let food be your medicine, and medicine your food
(Hippocrates).*

*"What we eat and drink has an important bearing upon our lives and characters"
(Ellen White).*

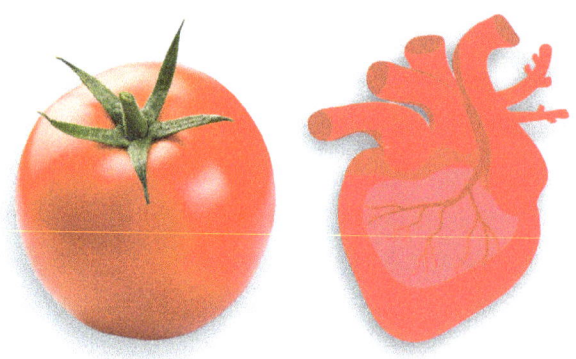

TOMATOES help keep your heart healthy, and they have four chambers just like the **HUMAN HEART.**

WALNUTS are excellent brain food. It is no surprise that the shape and wrinkles of a walnut make it look like a tiny **BRAIN.**

 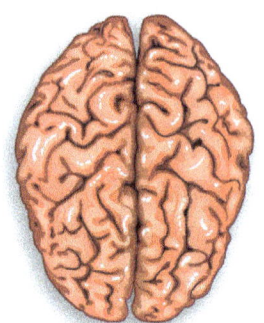

 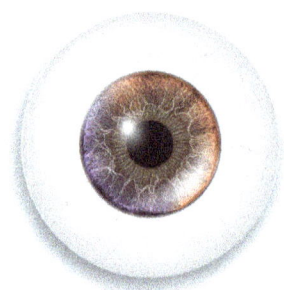

A sliced **CARROT** looks like an orange eye. The vitamin A in carrots supports healthy **EYES.**

KIDNEY BEANS help keep blood pressure low and regulate blood sugar. This is good for **KIDNEY** health.

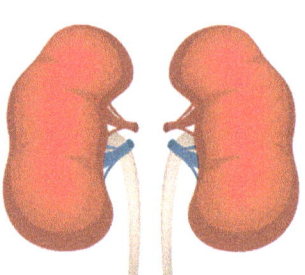 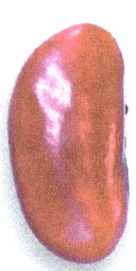 

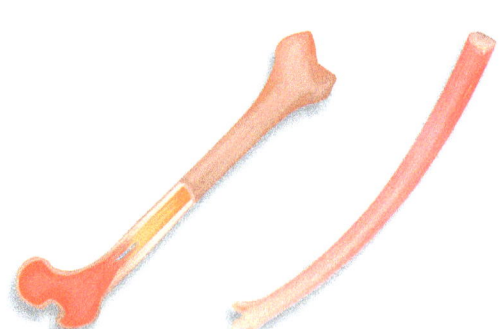

A stalk of **RHUBARB** looks like a **BONE.** It contains nutrients that support both bone building and bone strength.

Cooking Steps to Follow

Step 1. Say a prayer, because you need wisdom to cook, and because it is a special science.

Step 2. To enjoy a meal, you must enjoy where you prepare that meal. So, declutter your kitchen. Get rid of those things you have in your cupboards and drawers that you never use. Organize what's left. Order in a kitchen saves time, adds flavor, and lightness to your day.

Step 3. This is going to be a good day in the kitchen because you are making a healthy start. Be positive. There is no greater wealth than your health.

Step 4. Experiment; don't be afraid of making mistakes. These recipes are not written in stone; experiment with them. You are a scientist with a lab coat apron; cooking is a *special science*.

Step 5. Give yourself time to learn as cooking improves the more you do it.

Step 6. Don't be in a hurry to come out of the kitchen; in Guyana, we say, "hurry, hurry, makes bad curry." Enjoy your kitchen.

Step 7. You know you are getting somewhere when people are eating all your food and commenting, "This is good." But remember, people are different and tastes are, too.

Equivalents

3 teaspoon	=	1 tablespoon (Tbs)
2 tablespoons	=	1 liquid ounce (oz)
16 oz	=	1 pint (pt) liquid or 1 pound (lb) dry
16 Tablespoon	=	1 cup (c)
2 cups	=	1 pint (pt)
2 pints	=	1 quart (qt)
4 cups	=	1 quart (qt)
1 tsp	=	1 teaspoon
1 lb	=	1 pound
2/3	=	two thirds
1/4	=	one quarter

"And God said, Behold, I have given you every herb bearing seed, which is upon the face of all the earth, and every tree, in the which is the fruit of a tree yielding seed; to you it shall be for meat" (Genesis 1:29). So the Bible (KJV) begins by calling fruit "meat." The word translated *meat* does not mean flesh foods, or foods from animals. But meat here means *food* or *fuel*.

Definitions of Less Common Ingredients

Agar-agar	Dried seaweed used for thickening and gelling.
Carob	Healthful chocolate substitute that can be bought as a powder.
Coffee Substitute	Made from roasted grains: Caffix®, Pero®, and so on
Lecithin	Natural emulsifier (helps water and fats mix together well).
Sesame seeds	Sesame seeds, hulled is white, and has a milder flavor; brown is unhulled and is what is used in the recipes in this book.
Tahini	Butter made from sesame seeds.
Tofu	Mild tasting soft curd made from soybeans, it acts like a sponge and will take the taste of anything you put it into.
Turmeric	Yellow root that makes curry yellow.
Fine Whole Wheat Flours	A variety of white wheat flours that are a finer product, but completely whole wheat, for example, Prairie Gold® flour, a hard white spring wheat flour. These work better with pancakes, pastries, and mix well with straight whole wheat flour to give lighter textures to breads, etc.
Cumin	Herb also known as geerah (gives the flavor to curry)
Kelp	Seaweed that gives a certain seafood taste and smell to vegan dishes.
Gluten Flour	Protein found in flour. This is a high protein food and gives a chewy texture.
Annatto	A plant that bears a red seed, which is used for dyes and coloring. It is high in iron.
Okara	Byproduct of soy milk (the pulp of soybeans)
Barley Malt	Natural sweetener derived from barley

Carbohydrates

Best source of energy for all bodily functions:

> Brain
>
> CNS (central nervous system)
>
> Muscles

Comes from plant sources.

> Has half the calories as fat
>
> Fats 9 calories per gram
>
> Carbohydrates 4 calories per gram
>
> Proteins 4 calories per gram

Whole wheat is superior to refined and white products. One of the reasons for this is fiber—both soluble and insoluble fibers.

Benefits Of Insoluble Fiber

> Moves bulk through the intestines
>
> Gives regular bowel movement and prevents constipation
>
> Removes toxic waste through colon in less time
>
> Prevents colon cancer by keeping an optimal pH in the intestines to
>
> prevent microbes from producing cancerous products

Food Sources Of Insoluble Fiber

> Green beans, dark green leafy vegetables, fruit skins and roots, vegetable skins, wheat products, oats, corn bran, seeds, and nuts.

Benefits Of Soluble Fiber

> Prolongs stomach emptying time, so that sugar is released more slowly.
>
> Regulates blood sugar.
>
> Forms a gel in the intestine, binding to bile acids (when an insufficient amount of bile acids reach the liver, the liver converts the cholesterol present into bile acids, thereby reducing cholesterol levels)

Food Sources Of Soluble Fiber

> Oats and oat bran, dried peas and beans, nuts, barley, flaxseed, oranges, apples, carrots, psyllium husks

Breakfast Foods

Start your day with 3–5 pieces of fruit; these are the most important breakfast foods. Filled with antioxidants, they are what you need.

In the Caribbean we have quite a variety of fruits; use whatever is available in your location. It is better to buy fresh those fruits that are in season, but if all you have is canned or dried fruit, use it.

I like picking my own fruit fresh from the tree, if I can reach them before the toucan seen in the picture above does. They love their fruits. It takes a lot of energy to fly from tree to tree.

Pancakes

2 tablespoons applesauce
2 tablespoons honey
2 cups soy milk
1/2 teaspoon salt
1 tablespoon oil
1 cup flour
1/4 cup very fine cornmeal
1 teaspoon vanilla
1 teaspoon aluminum-free baking powder (optional)

Blend applesauce, honey, soy milk, salt, oil, flour, cornmeal, vanilla, and baking powder together, adding water to make it as thin or thick as you would like.

Pour onto a hot tawa or griddle.

If not using baking powder, place the batter into the freezer for 20 minutes before cooking, the cold mixture on the hot surface will cause it to rise naturally.

Granola

2 pounds rolled oats (about 4 1/2 cups)
1 3/4 cups sugar or 1 1/4 cup honey or maple syrup
1 tablespoon vanilla
1/4 teaspoon star anise powder
Juice of 1 sweet orange or 1/2 cup
2 ripe bananas
1/4 pound sliced almonds (about 1 cup)
1/4 pound sunflower seeds
1/4 pound pumpkin seeds
1/4 pound raisins
1 cup grated coconut
1 cup any dried fruit you like (bananas, berries, apples, etc.)

Melt sugar in a little water on the heat. If you are using honey or some other liquid sweetener, skip this part. Mash bananas; add sugar, vanilla, star anise, and orange juice. Add oats and stir mixture well. (You can use 2 or more mashed ripe bananas if you want a granola with more clusters.) Place mixture on two large cookie sheets. Put in the oven for 15 minutes at 350 degrees. Reduce to 250 degrees, stirring every 10 minutes for about 40 minutes, until almost done. Add almonds, sunflower seeds, pumpkin seeds, coconut, and dried fruit, except the raisins. Cook an additional 15 minutes. Turn off the oven, and add the raisins. Leave granola in the oven to dry out.

Breakfast Millet

(Porridge—One can replace any other grain with millet to produce this porridge.)

2 cups millet (it will swell)
1 box (32 ounces) soy milk
3 cups coconut milk or water
1/2 cup honey
1 teaspoon star anise
1/4 teaspoon cardamom
Pinch of salt

Place millet (or other grain), soy milk, coconut milk or water, honey, star anise, cardamom, and salt in a pot, and cook for at least 1 hour. Keep an eye on the pot because soy milk tends to boil over.

The trick to cooking delicious porridge is to boil your grain in the milk, honey and flavorings for the whole period until it's nice and thick and good. Do NOT cook the grain in just water, and then add milk when it's done. Try this with oats or even rice for a gluten free version. Or you can even use 2 cups of grated green plantain or cassava instead of the millet.

In Guyana, we use a lot of ground vegetables to cook porridges. If you are cooking a longer-cook grain, use a pressure cooker to cook grain in water until 3/4 way cooked. Follow the directions on the cooker accordingly. Add the milk and flavorings, and cook the rest of the way until finished.

Roti

1 pound flour
About 1 1/2 cups water
1/3 cup olive oil

Put flour in a bowl and add small amounts of water to make a soft dough. Divide dough into 5 equal parts. Place on a floured board, and roll out into a thin circle (1/4 inch thick). Spread 1 teaspoon of oil all over the circle, and sprinkle lightly with flour. Cut any part of it, from the middle to any part on the edge. Roll around clockwise as if forming a funnel or a cone. Press down the funnel or cone tip, and place in a floured bowl. Repeat for all five pieces. Let rest for one hour covered with a damp cloth. Now you are ready to make them. Oil a tawa (a flat iron cooking vessel). If you do not have a tawa, oil any flat pan or skillet. Roll out the roti dough again as you did the first time. Pick it up and lay it on the hot tawa or pan. Keep flipping it every 20 seconds, and brush it with oil at least once during cooking. Flip it about 5 or 6 times. Regulate your heat while it is cooking. In general, roti cooks on a medium to hot fire. When it is nicely brown, remove it from the heat. Lay it down on a paper towel for a minute, and clap it several times in the hand. If you cannot clap it because it is still too hot, then shake it in a container. It must be clapped hot, to gain the layers characteristic of roti. Repeat process for all other dough pieces. It is excellent with everything. Wrap in a damp cloth to keep soft.

BREAKFAST FOODS

Scrambled Tofu

1/2 cup finely chopped red sweet peppers
1/2 cup finely chopped onions
2 tablespoons oil (olive is best)
2 cups mashed firm tofu
1/2 teaspoon onion powder
1/2 teaspoon garlic powder
1/4 teaspoon salt
1/4 teaspoon turmeric
2 tablespoons fresh chopped chives or 1 tablespoon dried chives or parsley (optional)

Rinse tofu in cold water; drain and mash with potato masher or fork. In a skillet, sauté onions and sweet peppers. This process is not done with oil. It is a dry sauté, so watch the pan, so that nothing burns. Add tofu, onion powder, garlic powder, salt, turmeric, and chives, and stir together well on medium heat 5–10 minutes.

When it is done and cool, add olive oil. This way, and with almost all of the recipes in this book, you can have your food oil free if needed. Serve with bread, roti, and crackers, etc.

Baked Green And Yellow Plantain

Peel and cut green plantains as you would to make French fries. Add salt to taste and 1 tablespoon of olive oil. Place in a covered dish; bake at 350 degrees for 30 minutes. Take off the cover, and bake another 15 minutes. Cut very green plantains very thinly (paper thin). Add oil and salt, and bake for about 15 minutes at 400 degrees for crunchy plantain chips. Check them carefully to ensure they don't burn. Peel, and cut thinly ripe yellow plantains. Add oil and salt, and bake in an uncovered dish for 30 minutes at 350 degrees.

Sweeter Baked Yellow Plantains

4 ripe peeled plantains cut in halves
1/2 cup apple juice
2 tablespoons molasses
1 teaspoon coriander
1/2 teaspoon cardamom

Place plantains in baking dish. Mix apple juice, molasses, coriander, and cardamom together. Pour the mixture over the plantains evenly, and bake at 350 degrees for 30–45 minutes.

Hash Browns

6 large potatoes, shredded
1 teaspoon salt
1 cup walnut crumbs
1 large finely chopped onion
1 teaspoon garlic powder
1 teaspoon paprika
2 tablespoons sesame paste or tahini
1 tablespoon olive oil

Mix potatoes, salt, walnut crumbs, onion, garlic powder, paprika, tahini, and oil together. Press into patties, and place in an oiled dish that can be covered. Bake at 350 degrees for 30 minutes while covered. Remove the cover, and bake another 15 minutes until golden brown.

BREAKFAST FOODS

Breads

In my opinion, this is a very important food, and there are some secrets to good bread. Here they are:

1. Sweetener is key because yeast acts on sugars, raising the bread and making it lighter.
2. Kneading is key because it develops the gluten in the flour and leads to a softer bread.
3. Baking correctly so it doesn't fall is key, because nicely raised dough may still fall before it comes out of the oven.
4. Using a little yeast instead of a lot is key to having sweet smelling bread that is also light and good. Bread that smells like yeast is not appetizing.
5. Oiling the bread tops when your bread is done is key to its maintaining softness for many days.
6. Good bread takes time. Time is always key.

Basic Bread Dough

1 teaspoon yeast (this is not a typo, it is only 1 teaspoon of yeast)
1 cup honey or sugar
1/2 cup oil or homemade butter or applesauce
1/2 teaspoon salt
2 1/4 pounds flour (about 7 cups)
Approximately 2 cups warm water (hot water will kill yeast)

Place the flour and yeast into a bowl, and mix lightly. Add the sweetener, oil, and salt, and mix again. Slowly add the water, and stir together with a spoon. When it starts to pull together into a dough, it's time to use your hands. Knead dough for 20 minutes until your hands and your mixing bowl are clean of flour. Cover with a damp cloth, and let rise until double in size. Knead down again for about 5 minutes, and let rise until double in size a second time. Now knead down again and form into desired shapes, whether rolls or plaited, etc. Place in oiled pans, and let rise to double in size.

If you let your bread rise in your unheated oven as I do, do not remove the loaves, but light the oven at 100 degrees for 15 minutes. Raise it to 350 degrees for the next 20 minutes. Then reduce to 250 degrees, for a further 15 minutes.

If you let your bread rise on the counter, place loaves into a preheated 350-degree oven. Bake for 30 minutes, and reduce to 250 degrees for another 15 minutes.

When finished baking, remove pans from the oven, and brush all the tops with oil while the bread is hot.

Let bread cool 15 minutes in pans, and then take them out. This will help them to come out easily.

You can add raisins to this bread by plumping the raisins first, (by placing them in a pot with hot water for ten minutes, then straining.) Add the plumped raisins initially to the flour and mix well before adding the oil, sweetener, etc.

Tennis Rolls

1 tablespoon yeast
2 cups honey or sugar
1/2 cup oil or homemade butter
1 teaspoon lemon oil flavor
1/2 teaspoon salt
1 1/2 pounds flour

Follow as you would the above preparation, but form into little golf-sized balls. The lemon oil gives this roll a flavor that is irresistible.

Amadama Bread

1/2 cup fine yellow cornmeal (will not come out well with coarse cornmeal)
2 cups boiling water
2 tablespoons oil
1/2 cup molasses
1 teaspoon salt
5 cups flour
1 tablespoon yeast
1/2 cup lukewarm water

Place the yeast and 1/2 cup lukewarm water in a bowl for fifteen minutes so that a sponge is formed. Put the cornmeal and boiling water in a bowl for fifteen minutes; slowly add the oil, molasses, salt, flour, and the yeast sponge. This is somewhat sticky bread dough, but try to knead it as best as you can. Let rise until double in size. Knead again and form into loaves and place in bread pans. Allow to double in size. Bake in a preheated oven at 350 degrees for 40 minutes or a little longer until done. This is a heavier bread, but quite delicious to some.

Corn Bread

3 1/4 cups fine cornmeal
2 cups Prairie Gold® flour (or use some other white wheat)
1 teaspoon salt
1 tablespoon baking powder
2 cups soy milk
1 apple (remove seeds and purée)
1/4 cup honey
1/2 cup oil

Mix cornmeal, flour, salt, baking powder, soy milk, apple, honey, and oil together. Pour into a baking dish. Bake for 40–45 minutes at 350 degrees, until done.

Pinwheels

1 batch basic bread dough (page 22)
1 batch spaghetti sauce (page 61)
1 batch of prepared bulgur wheat*
1 batch of yellow sweet pepper cheese (page 62)
1/2 cup chopped string beans (bora)
1/2 cup chopped carrots
1/2 cup canned non-GMO corn kernels

Filling

Place carrots in a pan with 2 tablespoons of water and 1/2 teaspoon salt, and let them cook. Allow all of the water to dry out completely out of the pan. Add the bora or string beans, stirring constantly for a minute. Add the corn and the carrots to the prepared bulgur wheat. Roll out the dough into an 8x10-inch rectangle, 1/2-inch thick, the same as one does for cinnamon rolls. Spoon tomato sauce thinly onto rolled dough. Spread bulgur 1/2-inch thick onto the dough. Roll the dough up, and cut off 1 1/2-inch circles. Place on an oiled pan. Let dough double in size. Bake at 350 degrees in a preheated oven for 30 minutes. Take them out and spoon 2 tablespoons yellow sweet pepper cheese on top of each roll (or more if you like.) Place back into the oven and bake at 250 degrees for another 10–15 minutes until cheese is firm.

*Prepared Bulgur Wheat

Use 2 batches of the gluten sauce found on page 33. Add 4 cups of bulgur wheat to this and cook until completely dry. Remove from the heat. Add 4 tablespoons of olive oil, and allow to dry out overnight.

Coconut Rolls

Filling

2 cups grated coconut
1 cup honey
1 teaspoon cinnamon substitute
1 teaspoon star anise powder
1 teaspoon vanilla flavor

Dough

1/2 teaspoon yeast
3/4 cup honey or sugar
2 tablespoons oil
1/2 teaspoon salt
6 cups flour

Place coconut, honey, cinnamon, star anise, and vanilla in a pan and cook for 10 minutes, stirring frequently.

For this dough, use a white wheat flour, like prairie gold. Follow the same instructions as under basic bread dough. Roll out the dough into a rectangle about 1/2-inch thick. Spread filling evenly, about 1/4 of an inch thick. Sprinkle with raisins (optional). Roll rectangle into a log-shaped roll. Cut into 1-inch thick slices, and place cut side down into a baking dish. The baking dish should be 1/2 inch filled with coconut milk and 2 tablespoons honey. Pack them together, so that they will not open up. Wait until dough doubles in size. Bake in a preheated oven at 350 degrees for 40 minutes until golden brown. You can drizzle some white icing on top before serving.

Gluten Stuffed Bread

Filling

4 large ripe tomatoes, chopped
3 onions, chopped
1 whole bulb of garlic minced
I carrot, finely cut up
3 red sweet peppers, diced
1 tablespoon molasses
1 teaspoon salt
1 teaspoon thyme
1 tablespoon parsley
1 can green peas, drained
1 can corn kernels (non-GMO)

Place tomatoes, onions, garlic, carrots, peppers, molasses, salt, thyme, parsley, peas, and corn in pan and cook for 5 minutes. Add 1 1/2 cups of the prepared gluten, (See page 33) and cook another 10 minutes. Stir constantly, and cook on a medium fire to prevent burning.

One Batch Of Basic Bread Dough

Pull off pieces of the dough in tennis ball sizes, and stuff them with your filling. Close them back up, and place them seam-side down onto an oiled pan. Let the bread double in size. Bake, as you would basic bread. Delicious!

Pizza

Pizza dough*
Pizza sauce (page 60)
Yellow Sweet Pepper Cheese (page 62)
Bulgur or prepared gluten (page 33)
Toppings of choice (olives, onion rings, tofu cubes, peppers, spinach, etc.)

Roll out your dough, and spread a good amount of pizza sauce all over it. Gently pour on a thin layer of yellow sweet pepper cheese. Add your toppings, and spoon on the rest of your cheese. Bake at 350 degrees until cheese is firm, about 20 minutes.

Pizza dough*

1 1/4 cups warm water
3 tablespoons honey
1 teaspoons yeast
1 teaspoons salt
2 teaspoons oregano
1 teaspoons garlic powder
1 teaspoons onion powder
4 cups flour

Mix warm water, honey, yeast, salt, oregano, garlic powder, onion powder, and flour, and let double in size. Roll out on a flour dusted pizza pan or cookie sheet. Trim the edges and prick the dough with a fork. Bake at 350 degrees for 20–30 minutes, depending on how thin you made them.

Unleavened Bread (Communion Bread)

1 pound white wheat flour (about 3 1/2 cups)
1 cup olive oil
1 teaspoon salt

Mix the flour together with the oil and salt, and add a little bit of water at a time to make a soft dough. Roll out 1/4 of an inch thick. Score into cracker sizes, prick, and bake at 350 degrees for about 20 minutes until golden brown. (You can add a half-cup more oil, and 1 teaspoon of baking powder for nicer unleavened bread that also doubles as pastry crust).

Pine Tarts

Filling

1 large grated pineapple with its juice (about 4 cups)
2 tablespoons honey
Place in a pot and cook for 20 minutes. Stir halfway through.

Dough

1 batch of unleavened bread (see recipe above)

Roll out unleavened bread dough less than a 1/4 of an inch thick. Use a circular cookie cutter about 6 inches round (or just use the cover of a large jar) to cut out as many circles as possible. Brush each circle with honey. Spread some of the filling thinly over each circle. Don't put a lot near the edges or it will come out when you close it, but put instead 1 heaping tablespoon in the center. Don't spread this. Now fold in all three ends of the circle, pinching it together over the center to form a triangle. Brush the top with honey or milk, and set on a cookie sheet. Do this with all of the circles, and then bake at 350 degrees for 30 minutes.

Cheese Rolls

1 batch of unleavened bread dough
1 batch of yellow sweet pepper cheese (page 62)

Roll dough 1/4 of an inch thick, and cut into 4-inch by 4-inch squares. Spread cheese on your rectangle, but stay away from the edges by about half an inch. Now roll up the unleavened bread into a flat roll. With a fork, press the two sides down. Prick, and place on a cookie sheet. When your squares are filled, brush them with some soy milk, and bake at 350 degrees for 30 minutes.

Crackers

1/3 cup oil
1/3 cup cashew nuts
1/3 cup water
1/3 cup honey
1/4 teaspoon salt
1 1/2 cup flour
1 tablespoon baking powder

Blend oil, nuts, water, and honey until you get a smooth butter. Place salt, flour, and baking powder in a bowl, and mix with the butter. Mix well, until a big soft ball of dough is formed. Roll out less than a 1/4 of an inch thick. Score, prick, and bake in a preheated oven at 300 degrees for about 20 minutes.

Sesame Sticks

1/2 cup water
6 tablespoons oil
1/2 teaspoons salt
2 cups flour
1/2 cup sesame seeds
1 teaspoon garlic powder
1 teaspoon onion powder
1 teaspoon turmeric powder
1 teaspoon cumin powder (geerah)

Blend water, oil, and salt. Add flour, sesame seeds, garlic powder, onion powder, turmeric, and cumin. Mix well and knead a little. Let rest 10 minutes. Divide into 2 parts, and roll between waxed paper. Sprinkle with extra salt and sesame seeds to taste. Continue rolling to wafer thinness. Prick and mark squares. Bake at 250 degrees for about 15 minutes.

Flax Millet Crackers

1 1/2 cups millet flour
3/4 cup buckwheat flour
1 cup ground flaxseed
2 tablespoons maple syrup
1/4 cup almond butter
1 teaspoon salt
1/2 teaspoon coriander
About 3/4 cup soy milk
1 tablespoon caraway seeds (optional)

Mix millet flour, buckwheat flour, flaxseed, syrup, almond butter, salt, coriander, and soy milk. Roll dough 1/8-inch-thick, sprinkle with caraway seeds, and press them down with your rolling pin. Bake at 250 degrees for 45–60 minutes until crisp.

Flaxseed Crescents

Dough

1 cup warm soy milk
1/2 cup oil
1/2 cup honey
1 1/2 teaspoons salt
3/4 cup flax gel with flax seeds
1 tablespoon yeast
4 cups fine whole wheat flour
1 1/2 cups Bronze Chief® flour (ordinary whole wheat/hard red spring wheat)

Filling

1/2 teaspoon cardamom
1 teaspoon star anise
2 teaspoons agave
1/4 cup flaxseed gel
1/4 cup oil

Mix cardamom, star anise, agave, flaxseed gel, and oil together in a separate bowl and put aside. Mix soy milk, oil, honey, salt, flax gel, yeast, and flours into a dough, and let double in size.

Separate into two balls about 1/2 inch thick. Cut out triangles as big or small as you would like your crescents to be. Use a brush to apply filling thinly. Roll crescents from the base up to the triangle's point. Lay point side down on a greased cookie sheet. Brush with some milk. Allow to double in size. Bake at 350 for 30 minutes until done. *For a savory crescent, use cheese sauce as your filling instead.*

Flaxseed Gel

4 tablespoons flaxseeds
2 cups water

Place flaxseeds and water into a pot. Boil 5 minutes. Pass through a strainer for a clear gel or use as it is.

Meh Pot

Caribbean flava in de pot;

Girl come look, come smell,

Yuh gon get nice at dat.

Roti and curry, eddoe leaf and ackee.

Boy it good, leh me tell you wat;

No meat, but de food real sweet

Me put meh foot in um,

Before I leh it pass through meh teet.

Call all yuh neighbors dem,

We throw in down vegan to a Caribbean beat.

My mom and I were doing a cooking school in AR in the USA. My mom has taught me so much in cooking and in life and I just want to dedicate this book to her. She is a far better cook than me any day.

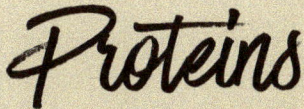

Proteins

Proteins are long chains of amino acids that do a lot of different things in the body, some of which are listed here:

1. They are involved as precursor elements.
2. They play a part in cell maturation.
3. They play a part in the formation of enzymes.
4. Hormones e.g.— thyroid hormone has the amino acid tyrosine.
5. Antibodies are made from amino acids by the lymphocytes.
6. B vitamin Niacin has tryptophan (amino acid).
7. Hemoglobin and myoglobin (which are involved in the blood) contain globular amino acids. Proteins are the second most abundant substance in the body. Only water is more abundant. As such, we do need protein, but contrary to popular opinion the vegan has no problem gaining enough protein, as you saw with those elephants and horses. Quite the opposite is of concern to me, as it seems evident that the normal flesh eater is eating far too much protein for his own health. And further, there seems to be systematic media warfare upon the mind, no doubt supported by the multi-billion dollar meat industry, to scare the public into believing that we all need more protein. And if we don't get it, we will have all sorts of health problems. The WHO (World Health Organization) recommends a daily allowance of protein of 50 grams, which science is proving is still too much. But regardless of this fact, if you check out the picture below, the average person is still consuming twice as much on most days. This picture talks about the average American diet, but is not this diet becoming the normal Caribbean diet? Are we not leaving off our ground provisions, and our fruits and mostly consuming KFC™, Church's™, and the other fast foods now? It seems that as goes America, so goes the rest of the world, and also the diseases that plague America. Could it be that our diet is affecting our health? Increased protein intake is not good. These are some of the problems associated with *too much* protein:

- Increased risk of osteoporosis, & CHD (Coronary Heart Disease)
- Accelerated aging
- More kidney stones
- Lowered immunity
- Increased risk of various cancers
- Increased ammonia and urea formation, which taxes the liver
- Nephritis
- Lowered endurance
- Increased periodontal disease
- Increased difficulty losing weight
- Raised cholesterol levels (Interestingly, this is only observed with animal proteins, but cholesterol levels lower with plant proteins.)

Enter The Essential Amino Acids

So here is the only concern for vegans on the protein subject. There are certain amino acids that our bodies do not produce; as such we need to consume them. But this concern causes no great difficulty, as long as we follow the first law of nutrition, namely VARIETY. As long as the vegan eats a variety of foods, he or she will have no problem gaining all the essential amino acids. The following is a chart of a variety of plant foods and their amino acid concentrations as compared with the recommended allowance.

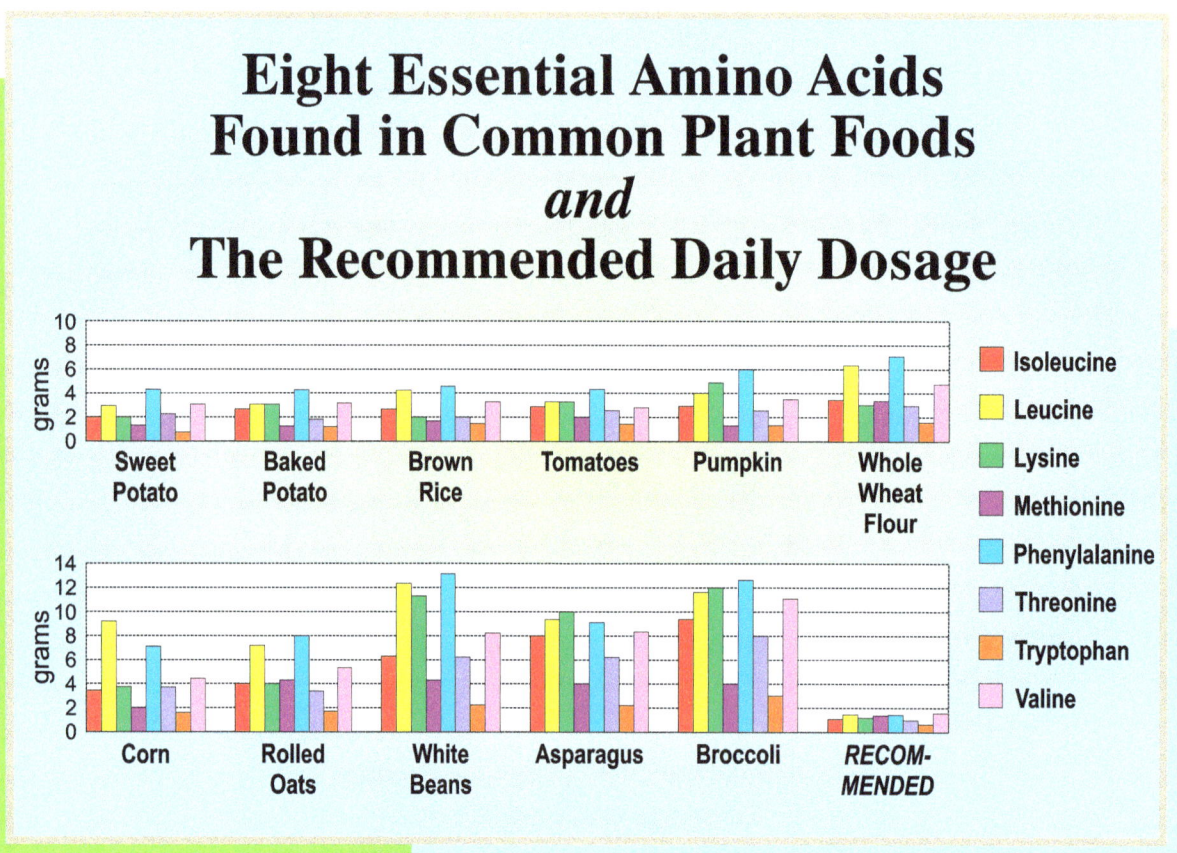

Entrees

31

Macaroni with Vegan Cheese

1 box (12 ounces) whole grain pasta
1 batch yellow sweet pepper cheese

Boil 2 packs of macaroni according to the directions on the package. Set aside. Pour this cheese over macaroni, mix well, and place in a baking dish. Bake at 350 degrees for 25 minutes. Before baking, you can crush blue corn chips over your dish—it adds flavor and beauty to the dish.

Baked Katahar or Jack Fruit

1 green katahar or jack fruit
1 batch of batter (page 62)
1 batch seasoned bread crumbs (page 66)

Cut katahar in pieces. I like cutting them like chicken nuggets. Smother them in the batter, and place them into breadcrumbs. Place them on an oiled cookie sheet. Bake at 350 degrees for 30 minutes. Serve them with anything, because they are just yummy!

Green and ripe katahar and jackfruit are not the same. When a katahar ripens, it produces a seed that looks similar to a chestnut. They are called breadnuts. Not to be confused with breadfruit which is a whole different fruit, and completely different taste, but the tree looks like a katahar tree. The seeds of the ripe katahar are boiled in salt and water and eaten. They taste similar somewhat to boiled peanuts.

When the jackfruit ripens, it has a rubbery yellow flesh around the seed, which is the only part that is eaten. Keep in mind that this fruit is the largest in the world. When ripe it is incredibly sweet. After taking off the pieces of flesh around the seeds, you can eat it as is, or you can bake it, and it tastes like baked yellow plantains. Or you can add about seven pieces to any puddings or creams or smoothies you like, and it will give a gum effect.

If handling either the green or ripe fruits use a pair of gloves and save yourself some of the clean up trouble if you handle it bare handed.

Gluten Tofu Loaf

2 cups extra firm tofu
3 cups soy milk
4 tablespoons toasted sesame seed oil or tahini
1 cup bread crumbs
1 tablespoons onion powder
1 teaspoon garlic powder
2 tablespoons sage
4 tablespoons molasses
1 tablespoon salt
1 teaspoon turmeric
1 teaspoon allspice
1 teaspoon coriander
1 teaspoon marjoram
1 teaspoon rosemary
1 teaspoon basil
1 teaspoon thyme
1 teaspoon star anise
1 teaspoon paprika
3 cups gluten flour

Place the tofu, soy milk, and oil in a blender. Blend until smooth. Add the breadcrumbs, and onion powder, garlic powder, sage, molasses, salt, turmeric, allspice, coriander, marjoram, rosemary, basil, thyme, star anise, and paprika. Place blended mixture into a bowl, and add the gluten flour a little at a time. The last of the flour will probably have to be kneaded in by hand. Pack tightly into a covered container, and place in a pot of boiling water. Let container boil for 30 minutes. Place in pan. Bake at 300 degrees for 40 minutes.

Prepared Gluten

2 pounds flour (about 6 1/2 cups)
water (about 3 cups)
1 teaspoon salt
4 tablespoons oat or wheat bran
1 tablespoon molasses
1 tablespoon roasted sesame oil or olive oil

Gluten Sauce

1 10-ounce can tomato paste
3 large onions
1 whole bulb of garlic
1 tablespoon thyme
1 tablespoon sage
1 tablespoon basil
1 tablespoon marjoram
2 teaspoons salt
2 tablespoons molasses

Place flour in a bowl and add water slowly to form a very stiff dough. Place dough in a bowl, and fill the bowl with water to cover the dough. Let the dough rest in water for 2 hours. Now place your dough in a large colander under the faucet in your sink. Let the water continuously run over your dough as you wash it, as you would wash a piece of clothing. The water will appear white at first. When it is no longer coming white but it is clear, you may stop, you have gotten rid of most of the starch, and there is a gluey piece of gluten left. Divide your gluten into about 1-inch pieces by pulling them apart bit by bit, creating your own vegan chunks. Pour over them the salt, oat or wheat bran, molasses, and roasted sesame oil or olive oil. Mix thoroughly. Place on a cookie sheet, and bake at 400 degrees for 30 minutes.

Blend tomato paste, onions, garlic, thyme, sage, basil, marjoram, salt, and molasses with 4 cups of water. Place your baked gluten chunks into this sauce after baking, and cook until sauce is dried up. Let cool and keep a batch of it in your freezer. The gluten will absorb all of the sauce and become loose. This is your prepared gluten, and it can be recooked now in many ways as a meat substitute.

Eggplant Stew

4 cups finely chopped eggplant
2 diced tomatoes
2 diced onions
8 grated garlic cloves
5 chopped dates
1 tablespoon marjoram
1 tablespoon basil
1 teaspoon salt
1 tablespoon olive oil

Place tomatoes, onions, garlic, dates, marjoram, basil, and salt into a pan, except the eggplant and the oil. Sauté all together, until onions are tender. Stir constantly. To sauté without oil requires attention. Add eggplant to pan, and mix all up, cook further until the eggplant is tender. When the dish is cool, add the olive oil. Serve with rice or bread, etc.

Baked Fries

8 medium potatoes
2 teaspoons salt
1 tablespoon olive oil
1 tablespoon grated garlic (optional)

Cut the potatoes into French fries, and mix them with the salt, oil, and garlic. Bake for 20 minutes at 350 degrees in a covered dish. Uncover the dish, and let them cook another 20 minutes until nicely browned. You can do the same thing with yams. Mmmmmm!

Pigeon Peas Stew

1/2 cup cooked pigeon peas
1/2 cup chopped onions
1/2 cup fresh chopped parsley
2 bay leaves
1/4 cup chopped string beans
1 teaspoon paprika
1/4 teaspoon salt
4 tablespoons soy milk
1 tablespoon olive oil

Place pigeon peas, onions, parsley, bay leaves, beans, paprika, salt, and soy milk in a pan, and cook everything for 5 minutes. Add olive oil when cool.

Colored Rice

1 cup rice
1 quart water

Add a little beet juice while cooking for red rice or a little turmeric or saffron powder for yellow rice.

Try using 1 cup red rice, 1 cup yellow rice, 1 cup black rice, and 1 cup white rice, for a colorful rice dish. You may add a few seasonings like garlic, basil, etc. to the rice. Serve with beans and vegetables.

Okara Fish Cakes or Fingers

8 ounces okara
7 ounces cooked, mashed yams
1 tablespoon oil or cashew butter
2 tablespoons chopped shallot
2 tablespoons chopped celery
1 tablespoon lemon juice
1 sweet red pepper, diced
Pinch of star anise
1 tablespoon dulse or kelp powder
6 cloves garlic, grated
1 onion, chopped
1 1/2 teaspoon salt
4 ounces dried seasoned bread crumbs (page 66)
1/2 cup flaxseed gel

Mix together the okara, yams, oil, shallots, celery, lemon juice, sweet pepper, star anise, dulse or kelp powder, garlic, onion, and salt. Place the mixture on a floured board. Make a roll 1 1/2 inches round. Cut in pieces to make fingers, or press down to make cakes. Coat with flaxseed gel then roll in seasoned breadcrumbs. Place on a tray and bake at 350 degrees, for 15 minutes. Turn and bake further 7 minutes on each side until a nice brown color appears.

Oatmeal Patties

2 cups rolled oats (pre-soaked in 4 cups hot water for 1 hour)
1 cup ground walnuts
1/4 cup ground pumpkin or sunflower seeds
1 small cooked, mashed eddo, yam or potato, or beetroot (about 3/4 cup)
1/2 cup thick soy milk
2 teaspoons salt
1 teaspoon sage
1 tablespoon molasses
2 tablespoons tahini or ground sesame seeds
2 onions
2 large red sweet peppers
1/2 cup chopped pineapple

Finely dice and sauté onions and peppers in a dry skillet. Don't use any oil. Stir continuously so as not to burn. Remove from heat and mix together the oats, walnuts, pumpkin or sunflower seeds, eddo, potato, or beet, soy milk, salt, sage, molasses, tahini, and pineapple. Form into patties. Bake in oven 45 minutes at 350 degrees. Flip halfway through to brown both sides.

Lasagna

1 package (8 ounces) lasagna noodles, cooked
3 cups yellow sweet pepper cheese sauce (page 62)
3 cups pasta sauce
3–4 cups prepared bulgur wheat (depends on how thick you want this layer to be, see page 23)
8-ounce package tofu, crumbled
Vegetables of your choice (optional)
3/4 cup seasoned bread crumbs (page 66)

Prepare a 9x12-inch oiled pan. Sprinkle all the seasoned breadcrumbs on the bottom of the pan. Spoon a thin layer of pasta sauce onto the breadcrumbs. Place one layer of pasta, and add more pasta sauce. Sprinkle bulgur wheat on top of that, then crumbled tofu on top of that, and finally yellow sweet pepper cheese on top of that. Repeat this and continue layering until you reach the top of your dish. When you reach your last pasta piece, put on pasta sauce, tofu, and yellow cheese. Now bake at 350 degrees for 30–40 minutes. (Instead of using lasagna pieces one could use eggplant of 1/4-inch slices that have been baked for 20 minutes. This would make it Eggplant Parmesan; it's quite delicious.)

Potato Pie

2 pounds cooked, mashed potatoes
1 can non-GMO corn
1 can mung beans
1 cup pre-steamed broccoli
1/2 cup onion
1 cup pre-steamed spinach
1/2 cup seasoned bread crumbs (page 66)

Layer potatoes 1/4 of an inch thick on the bottom of an oiled pan. Layer corn, mung beans, broccoli, onion, and spinach. Cover the greens with the rest of the potato, and sprinkle the top with breadcrumbs. Bake for 30 minutes at 350 degrees.

Roasted Eggplant Rolls

2 medium eggplants (sliced into 1/4 inch slices)
2 tablespoons lemon juice
1 teaspoon olive oil
6 tablespoons white cheese
1 green onion
4 sun-dried tomatoes
1 garlic clove
1/4 teaspoon oregano
16 fresh steamed spinach leaves
1 cup pasta sauce

Mix the lemon and oil together and brush the eggplant with this mix on both sides. Place eggplant on an oiled cookie sheet as a single layer. Bake 20 minutes at 450 degrees. Turn once halfway through baking, so that both sides are golden brown. Stir together cheese, green onion, tomatoes, garlic, and oregano. Put 1 teaspoon of mixture on the now baked and cooled eggplant slice. Top with a spinach leaf and roll up. Lay rolls on a platter as you go, seam side down. Serve with spaghetti sauce.

Curry Katahar or Jackfruit or Potatoes

Get a young green katahar or jackfruit. Peel it, and then cut it into small chunks, about 1 inch by 1 inch. (Or you can buy a can of cut chunks). Either way, you will need about two cups for this recipe. If you can't find katahar or jackfruit, then use potatoes instead. The other ingredients are:

2 tablespoons curry powder
7 grated cloves of garlic
1 grated onion
2 grated sweet red pepper (this is the secret of a good homemade curry, it must be grated finely like a paste)
1 teaspoon salt
3 cups fresh coconut milk or canned coconut milk

Place curry powder, garlic, onion, pepper, and salt into a dry pan. Cook this mixture until brown, stirring constantly. An aroma must fill the room, an aroma of curry (this takes about 3–5 minutes). To this dry roasted mix, add the coconut milk and the chunks. Cook for 20 minutes until the chunks are soft. You can choose to dry the coconut milk down completely or to leave some as curry sauce. This just depends on how you like it. It goes well with roti. This recipe is typical to curry anything. You can use tofu chunks or potatoes instead, or whatever you wish. In Guyana, we curry everything. We curry pumpkin, spinach, etc.

Mashed or Cubed Provision (Ground Vegetables)

4 cups provision of choice (my favorite is eddoes)
1 large onion diced
6 cloves grated garlic
1 teaspoon thyme
1 tablespoon scallions (shallot)
1 teaspoon salt
2 tablespoons oil

Peel eddoes (or provision of your choice). Wash, and cut up into cubes. Place in a pot with water that just covers them, and add salt. Let boil until the cubes are soft. Keep them this way or mash them. Remove them from the heat. Add onion, garlic, thyme, scallions, salt, and oil while provision is still hot, and mix well. If serving your provisions mashed, you can add 1/2 cup of milk during mashing.

In Guyana many root vegetables are called provision. So provision could be eddoes, cassava, sweet potatoes, yams of all sort, and breadfruit, which is the exception to the ground rule, as it grows on a large tree.

ENTREES

Burgers

Prepared Bread

1/2 batch of bread dough (page 22)

Filling

Oatmeal patties or okara fish cakes (or any other meat substitute you wish)
Scrambled tofu
Lettuce
Sliced tomatoes
Guacamole
Sliced olives
Lime Pickles
Onion rings
Diced sweet yellow pepper
Pineapple chunks

Follow the same method shown for basic bread, but make burger rolls. These are wide, flat rolls. Or simply use bread slices as pictured.

Set the substitute meat in the bread. Place bowls with various vegetables and other toppings, so that everyone may choose what they like, topping it off with a dressing, sauce, or ketchup, etc. The above is an example filling, but you can use any veggies you like.

If you are going to pack a burger to take with you, place bread and burger patty on a piece of wax paper, so that after you've filled it with the toppings of your choice, you can press it down and wrap it, before placing it in a bag. This will make it easier to pack and easier to eat.

Spinach Quiche

1 batch yellow cheese (page 62)
8 cups steamed spinach, callaloo or even kale

Mix cheese and greens together. Pour into a baking dish. Bake at 350 degrees, until cheese is firm, about 20 minutes. You can do this dish as a pie instead with an unleavened bread crust at the bottom.

Meatballs or Burger Patties

(All meatballs can be formed as patties instead)

Version A

1 cup rice
1/2 cup water
1 cup mashed lima beans
1 cup ground walnuts
1/4 cup ground raw beets
1/2 cup peanut butter
1 teaspoon onion powder
1 teaspoon garlic powder
1 teaspoon celery seed
1 teaspoon marjoram
1 teaspoon star anise
1 teaspoon salt
1 tablespoon each of sage
1 tablespoon thyme

Blend rice with water. Pour into a bowl, add lima beans, walnuts, beets, peanut butter, onion powder, garlic powder, celery seed, marjoram, star anise, salt, sage, and thyme, and mix well. Use a scoop or your hands to form meatballs. Place on an oiled cookie sheet, and bake at 400 degrees, turning every 7 minutes until most of the balls are a nice brown color. Cook in spaghetti sauce or serve as it is.

Meatballs or Burger Patties (continued)

Version B

1 cup ground walnuts or pecans
1/2 cup ground sesame seeds
1 cup bread crumbs
1 package tofu
2 tablespoons oil
1/4 cup ground sunflower seeds
1 teaspoon onion powder
1 teaspoon garlic powder
1 teaspoon marjoram
1 teaspoon salt
1 teaspoon parsley
1 teaspoon basil
1 teaspoon oregano
1 tablespoon sage
1/4 teaspoon crushed rosemary
1 tablespoon flaxseeds
1/4 cup water

Blend the flaxseeds and water until seeds are thoroughly crushed. Place in a bowl, and add nuts, sesame seeds, bread crumbs, tofu, oil, sunflower seeds, onion powder, garlic powder, marjoram, salt, parsley, basil, oregano, sage, and rosemary. Mix well. Use a scoop or your hands to form meatballs. Place on an oiled cookie sheet, and bake at 400 degrees, turning every 7 minutes until most of the balls are a nice brown color. Cook in spaghetti sauce or serve as it is.

Version C—this is the raw version

1 cup ground walnuts
1/4 cup ground pumpkin seeds
1/4 cup ground sesame seeds
1/2 cup cashew or almond butter
1/4 cup oat bran
1/4 cup ground raw beets
1 medium onion, chopped
1/4 cup chopped scallions (shallot)
1 large grated or puréed sweet red pepper
1 teaspoon each of garlic powder
1 teaspoon marjoram
1 teaspoon salt
1 teaspoon parsley
1 teaspoon basil
1 teaspoon salt
1 tablespoon sage
1 tablespoon flaxseeds
1/2 cup water

Blend the flaxseeds and water until seeds are thoroughly crushed. Place in a bowl, add walnuts, pumpkin seeds, sesame seeds, nut butter, oat bran, beets, onions, scallions, red pepper, garlic powder, marjoram, salt, parsley, basil, salt, and sage, and mix well. Use a scoop or your hands to form meatballs. Heat through either on a low grill or oven. This will go well with raw vegetable pasta and a raw spaghetti sauce. Complete raw diets for a period, are very beneficial to help with certain diseases.

Zucchini Cakes

2 tablespoon finely chopped red onion
1 medium zucchini
1/2 medium peeled potato
1 teaspoon garlic salt
1 tablespoon olive oil
1/4 cup flaxseed gel
4 1/2 teaspoons dry seasoned bread crumbs
1 teaspoon fresh chopped dill

Place onion in a skillet. Dry sauté for 5 minutes, stirring constantly so that it will not burn. Shred zucchini and potato. Squeeze dry in a paper towel. Combine onion and garlic salt, oil, flaxseed gel, bread crumbs, and dill with the zucchini and potato. Drop 4 heaping 1/4-cupfuls of mixture onto an oiled cookie sheet. Cook fifteen minutes at 400 degrees. Turn and cook a further ten minutes.

Basil Rice

3 cups brown rice or black rice
3 cups fresh basil leaves or 1 cup dried
Milk of 2 whole coconuts or 12–14 cups coconut milk
3 grated onions or 2 teaspoons onion powder
8 grated cloves of garlic or 2 teaspoons garlic powder
2 teaspoons salt
4 sprigs of fat leaf thyme

Place rice, basil, coconut milk, onion, garlic, salt, and thyme in a pot and cook until rice is done, about 45 minutes. This rice should be served with mango sour or cucumber sour. Best eaten the day after it is cooked.

When using fresh coconuts to make coconut milk, it is important to know that you can basically get as much or as little fresh milk as you need to cook your meal.

One coconut, after first blending gives you 2 and 1/2 cups of freshly squeezed milk. This is the creamiest. The residue of coconut is placed back in the blender twice more with water to give second and third extracts of milk. Theses extracts are far less creamy. When cooking certain meals like cook-up or basil rice in this book, plain water is never added to the dish. Milk is continually squeezed out of the coconut husk to get as much as is necessary to complete the meal.

Black-eyed Peas Stew

3 cups black-eyed peas
Milk of 1 coconut or 2 cups coconut milk
1/4 cup fresh basil or 2 tablespoons dried basil
1 teaspoon salt
2 tablespoons honey
2 chopped fresh tomatoes or small tin of tomato paste (optional)
1 grated onion or 1 teaspoon onion powder
4 grated garlic cloves or 1 teaspoon garlic powder
1/2 teaspoon sage
1/4 teaspoon thyme

Place black-eyed peas, coconut milk, basil, salt, honey, tomatoes, onion garlic, sage, and thyme in pot and cook until peas are done—45 minutes. If you want the peas to cook faster, soak them overnight. Serve with rice or bread.

Dahl

1/2 pint yellow split peas (about 1 1/2 cups)
1 teaspoon salt
4 cups water
1 tablespoon cumin
1 teaspoon coriander
1 grated onion
8 grated garlic

Soak split peas overnight. Place the split peas, salt, and water in a pot. Boil the split peas until soft and half dissolved. In a separate pan, place the cumin, coriander, onion, and garlic, and sauté them until the onion is soft. Add all your sauté to the soft split peas. Mix well. It should look like a lentil soup, but in Guyana, it is served with rice. You can add 1 tablespoon of olive oil before serving.

Split Peas Balls

2 tablespoons olive oil
1 cup split pea powder
1/4 cup flour
3 tablespoons cornstarch
1 teaspoon garlic powder
1 teaspoon onion powder
1/4 teaspoon coriander
1/4 teaspoon cumin
1/4 teaspoon paprika
1 teaspoon salt
1/4 teaspoon yeast
1/4 cup warm water
1 tablespoon honey

Place the yeast, water, and honey together into a bowl. Mix and let rise 15 minutes until bubbly. Place split pea powder, flour, cornstarch, garlic powder, onion powder, coriander, cumin, paprika, and salt in a separate bowl. Add the yeast mixture to all the other ingredients and mix well. You should have a stiff cookie dough consistency. Boil water (6 inches deep) in a medium-sized pot. When boiling, drop batter by spoonfuls into the water. Let boil 10 minutes. Remove and place in a colander to drain. When cool, use your hands to cover the balls with oil, or you can brush them. Place them on a cookie sheet and bake 15 minutes at 400 degrees. Eat with mango sour. Mmmmmmm!

Mashed Potatoes

4 large potatoes (about 4 cups)
1 teaspoon salt
1 large onion
3 cloves of garlic
1 tablespoon olive oil
2 tablespoons soy milk powder
1/4 teaspoon parsley flakes

Peel, chop and boil potatoes in about 4 cups of salted water. To your pot, add the garlic cloves whole and the onion chopped. When the potatoes are soft, turn off the heat. Do not strain, as the potato water will help give you fluffy potatoes. Add the soy milk powder, and begin to mash your potatoes right in your pot. Add the oil, and spend about 5 minutes mashing your potatoes. I use my potato masher to produce the mashed potatoes in a pattern. Then garnish with parsley. It's light, it's fluffy, and it's good!

Cassava Puffs

2 cassava pieces or 4 cups cassava
1 sprig fresh thyme or 1 teaspoon dried
1 grated or diced onion
6 cloves grated garlic or 1/2 teaspoon garlic powder
1 teaspoon olive oil
1 teaspoon salt
1 tablespoon molasses

Boil cassava until soft, and mash it as you would mash potatoes. Add thyme, onion, garlic, oil, salt, and molasses and mix well. Drop about 2 spoonfuls at a time on an oiled cookie sheet. Bake at 350 degrees for 30 minutes.

Cook-up

3 cups brown rice or wild rice
1 1/2 cups split peas (they need to be un-soaked and uncooked)
1 cup pre-cooked chickpeas (any peas or beans can be replaced here, e.g. black-eyed, red peas, etc.)
1 cup fresh basil or 2 tablespoons dried
1 cup chopped calaloo or spinach or eddo leaves
1/2 cup chopped pumpkin
2 teaspoons salt
1 teaspoon thyme
3 grated onions or 2 teaspoons onion powder
8 grated cloves of garlic or 2 teaspoons garlic powder
1/2 teaspoon coriander (optional)
Milk of two whole coconuts or 10 cups coconut milk

Place rice, split peas, chickpeas, basil, greens, pumpkin, salt, thyme, onion, garlic, coriander, and coconut milk in a pot, and cook until done. Usually takes 45 minutes to 1 hour. The dish should not be too mushy, and when cooled for a few hours or overnight, it should be loose. Serve with steamed vegetables.

Pak Choi or Bok Choy Stew

1 large onion, chopped finely
2 tomatoes, chopped finely
4 grated garlic cloves or 1/2 teaspoon garlic powder
1 teaspoon salt
1 tablespoon basil
1 cup coconut milk (optional)
6 pokchoi leaves

Cut off the white stems of the Pak Choi, and finely dice them. Place them in a bowl. Cut up the leaves of the Pak Choi finely and place them in another bowl. Put the onion, tomatoes, garlic, salt, and basil into a pan, and cook until onion is transparent. Add the coconut milk and the Pak Choi stems. Let cook until dry. Then add the Pak Choi leaves and cook them until they are how you like it. In Guyana, we stew all our vegetables in this way. In my country you can find pumpkin stewed, eddoe leaf stewed, calaloo stewed, squash stewed, and even corilla (bitter melon) stewed. The coconut milk is optional, but stews taste much better with it.

Channa

1/2 pint garbanzos
1 onion, grated
4 cloves of garlic, grated
1 tablespoon crushed dried celery leaf
1/4 teaspoon coriander
1/4 teaspoon cumin

Cook beans until soft and lay aside. In a pan place onion, garlic, coriander, and cumin, and sauté for about 2 minutes, stirring constantly. Add this and the celery to the garbanzos. When cool, add 1 tablespoon of olive oil. Mix together. This goes very well with chutney or sour (as is in the dressings section).

Ackee

2 sweet red peppers
2 sweet green peppers
1 medium onion
1 medium tomato
1/4 cup chopped scallions
1 teaspoon salt or less
1/2 teaspoon star anise
1/2 teaspoon basil
2 tablespoons honey (use when using ackee from can to balance the citric acid preserve)
1 can ackee

Dice the sweet peppers, onion, and tomato finely. Place them in a pan with the scallions, salt, star anise, basil, and honey. Cook for 3 minutes, stirring constantly. Open and drain ackee. Add to pan, but do not stir. Cook for another 3 minutes. Enjoy with anything.

Fats

Organic compounds that provide energy and insulation against shock and temperature. They are the structural components of cell membranes and are used to synthesize hormones and other molecules. We need fats but healthy fats.

ABOUT CHOLESTEROL:

Our liver makes all the cholesterol we need. As such you can only get extra or high levels of cholesterol by eating things that have a liver or a mother. Plant foods that don't have either a mother or a liver do not carry cholesterol. However, your body makes its own cholesterol in order to digest fats from any source. So while the vegan doesn't need to worry about cholesterol from meats, etc., he or she does need to remember to be temperate in all things. It takes 30 medium ears of corn to produce just 1 teaspoon of oil. So again, **temperance** with all fats and oils are needed. As a general rule, a handful of nuts, avocados, olives, etc. are a great source of fat.

UNDERSTANDING FRYING

Frying temperatures are more than 600-700 degrees F. Frying oils like olive or sunflower oil changes them from CIS to trans fatty acids, changing their arrangement of carbons and hydrogens, hence changing their chemical structure from bendable to straight. Thus, while a trans fat (fried fat) can be said to be unsaturated, example heated olive oil, etc., it behaves like a saturated fat. What is a saturated fat? We hear about them all the time; a saturated fat has been chemically changed to increase its stability and make it into a solid. All oils are liquid at room temperature. Even coconut oil which is a naturally saturated oil melts at room temperature. So here is the conclusion. Frying anything is not the best, and it is better to use fats that are liquid at room temperature. If the fat is solid at room temperature, it probably isn't very healthy for you.

RESULTS OF FAT DIGESTION.

1. Fats after a meal accumulate in arteries and capillaries reducing blood flow.
2. Fats in the blood alter the electrical charge on red blood cells, allowing them to clump together.
3. Excess polyunsaturated fats create free radicals, which cause oxidation.

This is the result of excess fat consumption, especially of bad fats, that is, those that are saturated, fried, and contain cholesterol, namely animal fats. Below right is a test tube of peoples' blood that has different levels of fat.

NOW ENTER ALL THESE OMEGA 3'S

The body makes its own fatty acids from carbon, hydrogen and oxygen molecules such as glucose, but there are two that are called essential because the body is not able to synthesize double bonds on omega 3 and 6. In simple words, your body needs for you to eat omega 3 and omega 6 oils. Most of us do well on omega 6s, which can be found in corn and sunflower oil. But we usually do pretty poorly on our consumption of omega 3s. However, they are found in walnuts and flaxseeds, etc. **But what about the fish factor**? Well, fish oils do contain omega 3s: however fishes have both a mother and a liver, so they come with cholesterol, as well as other things like mercury and other chemicals which tend to accumulate in their flesh through the process of bio-magnification. So the vegetarian/vegan is safer with his flaxseeds and walnuts. Use some of these every day. Make sure you grind your flaxseeds first, if not, they will simply provide fiber and pass through you.

Desserts

Carob Pudding

2 tablespoons carob powder
8 ounces soy milk or nut milk
2 tablespoons cornstarch
2 tablespoons honey
1 tablespoons vanilla extract

Combine carob powder, milk, cornstarch, honey, and vanilla in a medium-sized pan. Boil, stirring constantly until it gets thick. Chill and enjoy.

Carob No Cook Pudding or Soft Serve

1 cup avocado
1 sapodilla (remove seeds and skin)
1/4 cup dates (soaked for 3 hours, remove seeds)
1 tablespoon vanilla
1/4 cup virgin coconut oil
1/2 cup almond milk
2 tablespoons carob powder

Blend avocado, sapodilla, dates, vanilla, oil, milk, and carob powder, and place in a freezer for about 1 hour. Enjoy. (*If you can't find sapodilla, a sweet Caribbean fruit, then simply make the recipe without it.)

Carob Vs Chocolate
- Almost No Fat
- Fewer Calories
- 3 Times Calcium

Provides protein, natural sugar, B vitamins, calcium, magnesium, potassium, iron, manganese, copper, chromium, and nickel.

Sweet Loaf

2 cups white wheat flour
1 teaspoon salt
1 tablespoon baking powder
1/2 cup chopped walnuts
1/4 cup raisins
1/4 cup sweetened whole cherries
1/2 cup cashew cream
1/2 cup honey
1 tablespoon vanilla
1/2 cup mashed banana or apple-sauce
1/2 cup milk

Place flour, salt, and baking powder in a bowl, and add walnuts, raisins and cherries. Place the cashew cream, honey, vanilla, fruit, and milk in a bowl and mix well. Add the wet ingredients to the dry ingredients, and mix well. Place into an oiled loaf pan. Bake at 350 degrees for about 45 minutes until done. The red, sweetened cherries in this one make it so special!

Orange Cake or Muffins

1 1/2 cup white wheat flour
1 tablespoon cornstarch
1 tablespoon baking powder
1 tablespoon soy milk powder
3/4 cup honey
1 teaspoon orange flavor
1 tablespoon vanilla
1/2 cup water
1/2 cup almond or cashew butter

Blend the honey, orange flavor, vanilla, water, and nut butter, until smooth. Place in a bowl by itself. In another bowl mix together the flour, cornstarch, baking powder, and soy milk powder. Add the wet and dry ingredients together. Use a mixer to cream them together for about a minute or two. Pour into an oiled cake pan, or as I did, in muffin pans. Have the oven preheated to 400 degrees. Place the cake in the oven. After 5 minutes reduce the oven to 350 degrees for about 20 minutes until cake is done or until the toothpick comes out clean. These are beautiful muffins. They go well with frosting or a red cherry jam topping.

If you are using sugar in a cake recipe, use the same amount, but you may need to add some extra water or milk to get your cake consistency. Use this recipe for carob no-chocolate cake, by reducing the flour to 3/4 cup, adding 1/4 cup carob powder, and removing the orange flavor.

Coconut Ice Cream

1 can coconut milk (use a 13.6 ounce can that contains guar gum)
6 ounces cashew/ almond butter/ coconut oil
1 tablespoon vanilla
1/2 cup agave nectar
Pinch of salt
1 tablespoon lecithin (optional, but makes everything blend together easier)
1/4 cup non-dairy carob chips and/ or raisins (optional)

This coconut milk with the guar gum is thick like a coconut cream. Place it, as well as the nut butter or oil, vanilla, agave nectar, salt, and lecithin in a good blender. Blend well together. Place in a container. Add carob chips, mix in well, and refrigerate. This ice cream has the texture of ice cream. It is excellent. When frozen, you can take it out in scoops, or however you like. If you want a carob no-chocolate version, simply add another 6 ounces of coconut cream, and 1/2 cup of roasted carob powder to your blender.

DESSERTS

Ice Cream

1 teaspoon agar-agar
1/2 cup water
2 cups soy milk
1 cup cashews
1 cup tofu
1 teaspoon lecithin
1 cup honey
2 tablespoons vanilla
1 teaspoon guar gum or 2 teaspoons slippery elm powder
Pinch of salt

Dissolve agar-agar in 1/4 cup of water. Place in a pan to boil for about 1 minute. Place cashews and soy milk in a blender and thoroughly liquefy. Add tofu, lecithin, honey, vanilla, guar gum, salt, and the agar gel, and liquefy all together. Pour into a container. Freeze. Enjoy.

For a red or pink ice cream, use 1/2 cup strawberry or cherry juice to dissolve the agar-agar.

For a yellow ice cream, add a pinch of saffron when blending.

For fun variations, you can add raisins, carob chips, strawberry chips, banana chips, cherries, or blueberries to your ice cream when done.

Coconut Mango Ice Cream

3 large mangoes (remove seeds and purée.)
1/2 cup thick soy milk or cashew milk
1/2 cup honey
2 cups coconut cream
1 teaspoon vanilla

Mix mangoes, milk, honey, coconut cream, and vanilla well. Add to an ice cream maker, and follow the instructions.

Coconut Buns

3 cups white wheat flour
1/2 cup coconut oil or coconut cream
1/4 teaspoon salt
1 cup honey
3/4 cup grated coconut (or coconut flakes)
2 tablespoons applesauce
1 tablespoon vanilla
1 tablespoon soy milk powder
2 tablespoons baking powder

Mix flour, coconut oil or cream, salt, honey, grated coconut, applesauce, vanilla, soy milk powder, and baking powder together to make a stiff dough that can still drop from a spoon. Place by spoonfuls into muffin tins or onto a cookie sheet. Bake at 350 degrees for about 25 minutes. Can add 1/2 cup of plumped raisins to the batter for a little variation.

Cassava Pone

16 ounce grated cassava
8 ounce grated coconut
1/2 cup honey
1 tablespoon vanilla
1 teaspoon coriander
1/2 teaspoon cardamom
1/2 teaspoon salt
1 ounce oil (do not use olive oil for deserts, it changes the flavor)

Place cassava, coconut, honey, vanilla, coriander, cardamom, salt, and oil into a good blender, and add just enough water to make everything blend. It should be thick, not watery. Pour into a baking dish so that it is 1 1/2 inches thick. Set aside for 1 hour. Bake at 350 degrees for 30 minutes until the top and sides begin to brown. Cut into squares when cool.

Pumpkin Pone

16 ounces grated pumpkin with its juice
8 ounces cornmeal
4 ounces grated coconut
1 tablespoon vanilla
1 teaspoon star anise
1/2 teaspoon cardamom
1/2 cup honey

Combine pumpkin, cornmeal, coconut, vanilla, star anise, cardamom, and honey together. If your pumpkin doesn't have much juice, use 1/4 cup milk to mix all the ingredients together. Place into a baking dish 1 inch thick, and bake at 350 for 30 minutes. Allow to cool completely for 3 hours. Cut into squares and enjoy.

Sugar Cake

1 pound sugar
Orange peel
1 grated large coconut or 2 cups coconut flakes
1/2 teaspoon coriander
1/4 teaspoon cardamom

Add 1 cup of water to sugar and dissolve over heat. Add a 1/4 of the peel of a medium-sized orange. Boil until mixture comes to the consistency of a sling (or syrup). Remove orange peel. Add coconut, coriander, and cardamom. Continue to cook for about 15 more minutes, until mixture begins to become dry, and comes off from the sides of the pan. Place by spoonfuls onto a tray. Let cool, and it will be hard and ready to eat. This is a real treat, and in Guyana, we make it in different colors.

Guava Cheese

2 pounds guava (about 5 cups)
About 1 pound sugar or honey (about 2 1/4 cups)

Peel guavas and cut in halves, and remove seeds. Place in just enough water to cook until tender, and then rub the soft guavas through a sieve or fine strainer. Add 1 pound of sugar to each pint (about 2 1/2 cups) of pulp. Place in pot and boil till the mixture leaves the sides of the pot. Stir a while on the heat. Pour into a container an inch deep. Cut when cool. This was a childhood sweet treat. You can do the same thing with ripe mangoes; oh, it's delicious, too.

Conkie

Twine
Banana leaves or foil
16 ounces finely ground cornmeal
16 ounces grated or mashed pumpkin
6 ounces grated coconut
6 ounces soy milk
Honey to taste (about 6 ounces)
1 teaspoon salt
2 ounces cashew butter
1 teaspoon star anise
½ teaspoon cardamom
4 ounces dried fruit (optional)

Mix together cornmeal, pumpkin, coconut, soy milk, honey, salt, cashew butter, star anise, cardamom, and dried fruit. Add enough water to make a dropping consistency. Wipe banana leaves. Heat them a little by pressing them with an iron or passing them over a fire to make them more pliable. Cut the leaves into 8x8-inch pieces. Drop a little mixture into the leaf (about 4 heaping tablespoons). Wrap it in the leaf and tie with twine. Place in boiling water for 20 minutes. Use foil if you don't have banana leaves, but it will not taste exactly the same.

Fruit Cake

1/2 pound currants
1/4 pound raisins
1/4 pound prunes (without pits)
1 cup grape juice
1/2 cup oil
1 teaspoon vanilla
2 teaspoon coriander
1 teaspoon cardamom
1/2 cup honey
1 small apple (remove core and seeds)
4 cups flour
2 tablespoons cornstarch
1 tablespoon baking powder

Soak the currants, raisins, and prunes in the grape juice for 1 hr. Blend currants, raisins, prunes, juice, oil, vanilla, honey, and apple together. In another bowl place coriander, cardamom, flour, cornstarch, and baking powder. Add wet and dry ingredients together. Pour mixture into a cake pan. Bake at 350 degrees for about 40 minutes.

Frosting

1 cup soy milk or nut milk
1/2 cup cashews
1/2 cup agave
1/2 cup melted virgin coconut oil
2 tablespoons vanilla

Blend milk, cashews, agave, oil, and vanilla together until very smooth, until cashews are completely liquefied. Place in freezer 45 minutes, and whip as you would any whipped cream.

Rice Custard Tarts

2 cups leftover rice porridge (make the same as Breakfast Millet on p. 17)
1/2 cup honey
1 tablespoon vanilla
1 teaspoon lemon flavor
1 tablespoon oil
1 tablespoon soy milk powder
1 batch unleavened bread recipe

Filling

Take leftover rice porridge, and blend it with honey, vanilla, and lemon flavor. Use a little milk if needed to help it to blend smooth. It should be completely liquefied. Place mixture on the heat to boil and thicken until a soft fudge stage or a scoop stage. Turn off the fire, and stir in the oil and soy powder.

Shells

Make tart shells (shells shaped like a cup). Use the unleavened bread recipe. Roll out dough 1/4-inch thick. Cut into 4x4-inch squares, and form into cups by turning up sides. Place on a cookie sheet and bake until almost done. (You can also use individual pie crusts instead, or a big pie crust, and do it all in one shell as you would a cheesecake.) Fill the tarts with the filling, and bake again at 250 degrees until the top begins to brown. Truly delicious!

No Cook Dessert

1/2 cup honey
1/4 cup maple syrup
1 teaspoon orange extract
1/2 cup carob powder or soy milk powder
1/2 cup sesame seeds
1 cup chopped walnuts
1 cup chopped almonds
4 cup puffed grain

Add honey, maple syrup, and orange extract to a bowl. Slowly add in carob powder or soy milk powder by sifting it in. Add sesame seeds, walnuts, almonds, and puffed grain, and pack into a sprayed pan to freeze.

Frosting

1/2 cup raw cashews
1 tablespoon agar-agar powder
1 1/4 cups boiling soy or nut milk
1/2 cup honey
2 tablespoons lecithin
1 teaspoon lemon juice
1/4 teaspoon salt
1 teaspoon vanilla
1 tablespoon almond oil
1 cup coconut oil

Blend cashews, agar-agar, and milk until smooth. Place in a pot and boil 3 minutes. Place back into the blender. Add honey, lecithin, lemon juice, salt, vanilla, almond oil, and coconut oil, and continue blending. Pour into a dish and place in the freezer for about 20 minutes to set up. Remove from freezer and whiz in a mixing bowl. Use clearer honey for a whiter frosting.

DESSERTS

Raisin Oat Cookies

1 cup flour
1 cup ground oats
1 tablespoon almond flavor
2 tablespoon honey
1 cup applesauce (or 1 small apple peeled,
cored and blended)
1 1/2 cups plumped raisins

Whiz oats in a blender to make 1 cup of flour. Mix flour, oats, almond flavor, honey, applesauce, and raisins together. Drop by spoonfuls, and press down on a cookie sheet. Bake at 300 to 350 degrees for 20 minutes. Try substituting some carob chips instead of raisins.

Brownies

1/2 cup flour
1/4 cup oat flour or gluten flour
1/2 cup carob powder
1 tablespoon coffee substitute granules
(like Roma®)
1 tablespoon baking powder
1/2 cup honey
3/4 cup rich milk
1/2 cup cashew butter
1 tablespoon vanilla
1/4 cup carob molasses or date butter

Mix flours, carob powder, coffee substitute, and baking powder in one bowl, and honey, milk, butter, vanilla, and molasses in another. Mix both together and pour into pan. Bake at 350 degrees for 30 minutes. Top with a frosting, and you have a decadent dessert.

Pineapple Cheesecake

Crust

2 cups finely ground almonds and walnuts (at least—use more for a thicker crust).

Filling

1 ounce pineapple juice
2 teaspoons agar-agar
8 ounces tofu
1 cup cashew nuts
2 tablespoons vanilla
1/2 cup maple syrup
8 ounces sweet pineapple chunks
pinch of salt
1 teaspoon orange peel (optional)

Experiment with your crust, you can try different nuts, biscuits, or granola if you have them, or even the fudge recipe. Press down ground nuts into a freezer dish. Place in the freezer until filling is ready, about ten minutes.

Mix pineapple juice with agar-agar powder. Place in a pan, and heat until boiling. Place tofu, nuts, vanilla, maple syrup, pineapple chunks, salt, and orange peel along with the hot agar-agar in a good blender. Blend all together until very smooth. Pour mixture on top of the crust. Replace dish in the freezer for at least 4 hours before serving.

Mango topping

2 tablespoons pineapple juice
1 teaspoon vanilla
2 tablespoons honey
1 cup mango pulp

Blend juice, vanilla, honey, and mango together. Place in a pot. Cook for 5 minutes. Let cool. Pour on top of cheesecake when ready to serve.

Carob Fudge Topping

1 cup carob
1/2 cup coconut oil
3/4 cup honey
2 tablespoons liquid lecithin
1 teaspoon vanilla
Chopped coconut

Blend well the carob, oil, honey, lecithin, and vanilla. Add as much chopped coconut as you like, and put in the refrigerator. Pour on cheesecake when ready to serve.

DESSERTS

Key Lime Pie

Crust

1 cup granola or cookies or 1 cup pecans or almonds
1/4 cup cashews
1 tablespoon lime juice with zest
1/4 cup coconut flakes
1/4 cup maple syrup

Filling

2 teaspoons agar-agar powder
2 cups soy milk
2 large or 4 small avocados
3 tablespoons maple syrup
1 tablespoon vanilla

For crust recipe, grind the granola, cookies, or nuts, cashews, lime juice and zest, and coconut flakes together, adding the maple syrup last to hold it all together.

For your filling, mix agar-agar with soy milk and boil for 5 minutes. Blend mixture with the avocados, maple syrup, and vanilla until smooth. Press your crust into a flexible pan or a cake pan. Pour filling into it, and smooth down. Refrigerate for 3 hours. Can decorate however you like.

Raw Carrot Cake

3 cups shredded carrots
1 1/2 cups soaked dates
1/3 cup coconut flakes
1/3 cup virgin unrefined coconut oil
1 cup walnuts
Pinch of salt
1 teaspoon coriander
1/2 teaspoon cardamom
1 tablespoon almond flavor

Add carrots, dates, coconut, oil, 1/2 cup of the walnuts, salt, coriander, cardamom, and almond flavor to a food processor, and pulse until fine and well mixed like a cream. Fold into this, the remaining half-cup of the walnuts. Place in a pan in the freezer until it sets up. Serve with any frosting.

Frosting Cream

2 cups soaked cashews
1/3 cup water
1 teaspoon vanilla
1 tablespoon lemon juice
2/3 cup coconut oil
1/3 cup maple syrup

Blend cashews, water, vanilla, lemon juice, oil, and syrup, and refrigerate to set.

Peanut Butter Cookies

1 cup chunky peanut butter
1/2 cup honey
1/4 cup date butter
1/4 teaspoon salt
1 tablespoon vanilla
1 cup flour
1/4 cup oat flour

Cream the peanut butter, honey, date butter, salt, and vanilla together, and then add the flours. Form into flat round cookies with your hands. Bake at 250 degrees for 20 minutes.

Mom's Cookies

2 cups rolled oats
2 cups flour
1/2 cup plumped raisins
1/2 cup walnuts
1 cup honey
1 cup oil (don't use olive oil)
1 tablespoon vanilla
1 teaspoon coriander
1/2 teaspoon cardamom
1/4 cup hot water

Mix oats, flour, raisins, walnuts, honey, oil, vanilla, coriander, cardamom, and hot water together in a bowl, and leave for 30 minutes until oats have softened and the mixture is sticky. Form cookies by pressing some mixture into a jar lid about a 1/2-inch thick. Remove from the lid and place on an oiled cookie sheet. Bake at 300 degrees for 35 minutes.

No Bake Cookies

3/4 cup date butter
1/4 cup overnight soaked Brazilian nuts
1 cup wheat germ flakes
1/4 teaspoon ground anise seed
1 cup shredded coconut

Use a food processor to mix and grind date butter, nuts, wheat germ, anise, and coconut together. Form into cookies and refrigerate.

Carob No Chocolate Bars

1 cup coconut oil, (if you don't want the coconut flavor, use refined coconut or palm oil)
1 cup carob powder
1/2 cup honey
1 tablespoon lecithin
1 tablespoon vanilla
2 tablespoons barley malt (optional)
1/4 cup hazelnuts (optional)
1/4 cup raisins

Blend oil, carob powder, honey, lecithin, vanilla, and barley malt together. You will need a powerful blender, as the mixture will become very thick. I use an old Osterizer™ or a Vita-Mix™. When blending is done, stir in the nuts and raisins. Line a pan with a wax paper, pour into pan and freeze for 6 hours or overnight. This is my favorite dessert. For all past chocolate lovers, this is the caffeine-free, healthy, taste-like-the-real thing substitute. You may play with this recipe by adding shredded coconut, and pouring the mix into molds. Really, the sky is the limit with this one! Try different flavorings. Try substituting the carob powder for a milk powder instead, and adding carob chips for a white no chocolate bar with chips, or crushed carob cookies for a cookies-n-cream white no-chocolate bar.

(You can do this recipe with carob chips. If so, you will need to melt them and reduce the honey and oil in the recipe by half).

"Reece's"-like Fudge

1 cup carob powder
1 cup unsweetened soy milk powder
2 tablespoons non-alcoholic vanilla
1/4 cup honey
1/2 cup agave
3/4 cup chunky peanut butter
Pinch of salt
1/2 cup raisins (optional)

Sift the carob powder. Place carob powder, soy milk powder, vanilla, honey, agave, peanut butter, and salt into a bowl, and use a spoon to stir and mash everything together. When all is well incorporated, add raisins. Press the mixture into a freezer pan, and freeze for at least 30 minutes. You can eat it without freezing as well, because it's simply wonderful!

Candied Pecans

1 cup honey
1/2 cup cherry juice
1/2 teaspoon coriander, cardamom, or star anise
4 cups pecan halves

Bring honey and juice to a low boil to form a thick sauce (about 15 minutes). Take from heat. Add coriander or other spice and pecans. Stir for 10 minutes; pour onto waxed paper and separate. Let cool.

Fudgesicles

1 cup soy milk
3/4 cup chopped dates
3/4 cup walnuts
1/2 cup cashew cream
1 cup coconut oil (use refined coconut oil if you don't want the taste of coconut)
2 tablespoons toasted carob powder
1/2 teaspoon vanilla

Blend soy milk, dates, walnuts, cashew cream, oil, carob powder, and vanilla together, pour into a popsicle mold, and freeze. Place a stick in the center when half frozen, and continue to freeze.

Fudge

1 cup almond butter or cashew butter
1/3 cup honey
1 cup soy milk powder
1/2 teaspoon vanilla
1/2 cup chopped walnuts (optional)

Mix nut butter and honey well. Add the soy milk powder, vanilla, and nuts, and mix well. Spread in a pan 1 inch thick. Refrigerate until completely cold. Cut into squares.

Caramel Popcorn

1 cup popcorn
1/4 cup honey
1/4 cup peanut butter
1/4 teaspoon salt
1 tablespoon molasses

Pop popcorn, and place in a bowl. Place honey, peanut butter, salt, and molasses in a pan, and heat until all is nicely melted together, about 5 minutes. Drizzle mixture over the popcorn until well coated. Place on a baking sheet, and bake 1 1/2 hours at 200 degrees. Stir every 20 minutes. Let completely cool before serving.

Notes

Butters, Creams, Dressings, Etc.

Butter

1 cup olive oil
1 cup coconut oil
3 tablespoons lecithin
Salt to taste
Pinch of saffron for color (optional)

Blend oils, lecithin, salt, and saffron (if used) together and refrigerate. Will harden and be spreadable, but will melt at room temperature. (Refined coconut oil hasn't a coconut scent, and is preferable in this recipe; a normal coconut oil will make coconut butter.)

Date Butter

1 1/2 cup pitted dates
1 cup boiling water

Blend until smooth.

Dipping Sauce

1 cup coconut milk
1/4 cup water
1/2 cup creamy nut butter
2 tablespoons lemon juice
2 tablespoons honey
1 teaspoon coriander
1/8 teaspoon cayenne (optional)
1 teaspoon garlic powder
1 teaspoon onion powder
1 teaspoon marjoram
1 teaspoon sage
2 tablespoons chopped green scallions

Blend coconut milk, water, nut butter, lemon juice, honey, coriander, cayenne, garlic powder, onion powder, marjoram, and sage together. Add the scallions after blending.

Pizza Sauce

1 can tomato paste (16-ounce)
2 cups tomatoes
1 red sweet pepper
1 onion
1/4 cup lemon juice
6 tablespoon honey or sorghum
4 teaspoon oregano
1 teaspoon basil
1 teaspoon garlic
1 teaspoon onion
1/4 teaspoon thyme
1 teaspoon sage
1 teaspoon salt

Blend tomato paste, tomatoes, pepper, onion, lemon juice, honey or sorghum, oregano, basil, garlic, onion, thyme, sage, and salt, and cook for 10 minutes or until nice and thick like ketchup. Stir in 1 tablespoon of olive oil when cool. Or you may use as it is without cooking, depends on how thick you want your sauce.

Spaghetti Sauce

4 cups crushed tomatoes
2 cups tomato paste
1/2 cup soy milk (optional)
1/2 cup water
1 large onion, diced
2 tablespoons honey
1 tablespoon molasses
1 teaspoon salt
1 teaspoon oregano
1 bay leaf
4 tablespoons sweet basil
1 tablespoon lemon juice
7 cloves grated garlic
2 tablespoons olive oil

Cook tomatoes, tomato paste, soy milk, water, onion, honey, molasses, salt, oregano, bay leaf, basil, lemon juice, and garlic in a pot until desired thickness. Let cool, and then add the oil.

Spicy Sweet and Sour Sauce

1 diced green onion
1/4 cup honey
1 tablespoon cornstarch
3/4 cup rice water
2 tablespoons lemon juice
1/4 teaspoon ginger
1/4 teaspoon cayenne

Mix onion, honey, cornstarch, water, and lemon juice together in a pot. Boil for five minutes stirring constantly. When cool, stir in the ginger and cayenne.

White Cheese

1 tablespoon agar-agar powder
1/2 cup water
2 tablespoons sesame seeds
1 cup cashews
1 package tofu
1 teaspoon onion
1 teaspoon garlic powder
1 ounce lime or lemon juice
1 tablespoon olive oil
1/4 cup cooked garbanzos
1 teaspoon salt

Dissolve agar-agar in 1/2 cup water. Place on low heat, and cook for about five minutes. Place agar-agar mix, sesame seeds, cashews, tofu, onion, garlic powder, juice, oil, garbanzos, and salt into the blender. Blend all together using soy milk as needed. Pour into a bowl and refrigerate until cheese sets up

BUTTERS, CREAMS, DRESSINGS

Yellow Sweet Pepper Cheese Sauce

2 tablespoons sesame seeds
2 tablespoons olive oil
1 tablespoon water
1 1/2 cup chopped sweet red peppers
2/3 cup water
1 tablespoon onion powder
1 tablespoon garlic powder
1 tablespoon turmeric powder
1/3 cup lime or lemon juice (may need to use more if using lemons that aren't sour)
1 teaspoon salt
1/2 box or 6 ounces soft tofu
1 full cup raw cashew nuts

Blend the sesame seeds, oil, and water until smooth. Slowly add the peppers, water, onion powder, garlic powder, turmeric powder, lime juice, salt, tofu, and cashews, and liquefy until completely smooth. This is the cheese I use when making quiche or macaroni and cheese. This cheese can be made to be sliceable by doing the following: Dissolve 1 tablespoon agar-agar powder in about 3/4 cup water, and bring that to boil for about a minute. It will get thick fast, so watch carefully. Add the thickened agar gel to the cheese in the blender and blend again. Pour into a mold and place in refrigerator to set up.

Garbanzo Spread

1 tablespoon olive oil
1 cup cooked channa (garbanzo beans)
1 tablespoon sesame seeds or tahini
1 teaspoon onion powder (1 medium onion)
1 teaspoon garlic powder (or 6 garlic cloves)
2 tablespoons lime or lemon juice
1 teaspoon salt
1/2 teaspoon turmeric
1 cup soy milk
1 tablespoon non-GMO cornstarch (optional)

Blend oil, garbanzos, sesame seeds or tahini, onion, garlic, juice, salt, turmeric, milk, and cornstarch together until smooth. Put into baking pan. Bake 30 minutes at 350 degrees. You can replace the garbanzos in this recipe with any white peas.

Olive Spread

1 can of olives (black or green)
1/2 cup olive oil
1 cup cashew or sunflower seed meal
3 cloves garlic
salt to taste

Blend olives, oil, nut meal, garlic, and salt together.

Cucumber Relish

12 small cucumbers (about 15 cups)
2 onions
2 sweet peppers
4 ounces salt
8 ounces honey
1 teaspoon turmeric
1 teaspoon cayenne pepper
1 tablespoon celery seed or dill seed
1½ pint lime or lemon juice (about 3½ c)

Chop up cucumbers, onions, and peppers, and place them in a clean jar. Pour the salt, honey, turmeric, cayenne, celery seed or dill seed, and juice over the veggies, and shake well. Keep in the refrigerator. Add to salads, dishes, and stews etc.

Green Mango Sour

3 green mangoes
3 garlic cloves
1 teaspoon cumin
1 teaspoon salt

Peel green mangoes, and cut them up. Place them in a pot of water, where the water just covers them. Add garlic, cumin, and salt, and let cook until soft. Mash the entire mango, garlic and everything together in the pot. This is called sour, and it goes well with so many things. You will often see us eating it with plantain chips if you ever visit my country.

Cucumber Sour

1 whole large cucumber
2 tablespoons lime or lemon juice
1 teaspoon salt
3 garlic cloves
1 teaspoon cumin

Peel the cucumber, and remove seeds. Place cucumber, juice, salt, cloves, and cumin with a little water in a blender, and blend until smooth. Pour all in a pan and cook for 2 minutes. This is good too!

Homemade Ketchup

6 ounces tomato paste
4 ounces chopped tomatoes
2 tablespoons olive oil
2 tablespoons lemon juice
2 tablespoons honey
1 teaspoon lecithin
1 teaspoon garlic powder
1 teaspoon onion powder
1 teaspoon salt

Blend tomato paste, tomatoes, oil, lemon juice, honey, lecithin, garlic powder, onion powder, and salt together.

Salsa

4 whole tomatoes
4 tablespoons fresh cilantro or 2 tablespoons fresh culantro
4 finely diced tomatoes
1 can of tomato sauce (8 ounces)
1/2 cup diced sweet pepper or pimientos
Salt to taste
Lemon juice to taste
Cayenne pepper to taste
1/2 cup diced onion
1 tablespoon cumin
1 teaspoon basil
1 tablespoon olive oil

Blend the tomatoes and the cilantro. Place this along with the tomato sauce, pepper, salt, lemon juice, cayenne, onion, cumin, basil, and oil in a bowl, and mix well. Good for a fresh dip, or place in a jar and refrigerate.

Batter

3 tablespoons sesame seeds
1 cup water
1 tablespoon flaxseed
1 cup water
9 garlic cloves
1 tablespoon pineapple
2 tablespoons almond butter
1 teaspoon salt
3/4 cup flour
2 teaspoons marjoram
2 teaspoons thyme
2 teaspoons onion powder
1 tablespoon sage
1/4 teaspoon turmeric
1 tablespoon lime juice

Place the sesame seeds and water in the blender and blend until smooth. Empty into a bowl. Place the flaxseeds and water in the blender and blend until flaxseed is crushed and has gel-like consistency. Add the garlic and pineapple and blend until smooth. Place this in the same bowl that has the sesame paste. Add the flaxseed gel, almond butter, salt, flour, marjoram, thyme, onion powder, sage, turmeric, and lime juice to the bowl, and mix well. Makes about 3 cups.

Eggless Mayonnaise

1 cup tofu
1/2 cup cashews
2 teaspoons honey
1/2 teaspoon lecithin
1 teaspoon salt
1/4 cup lemon juice
1 1/2 teaspoons onion powder
1 1/2 teaspoon garlic powder
3/4 cup soy milk.
1/4 cup oil

Blend tofu, cashews, honey, lecithin, salt, lemon juice, onion powder, garlic powder, and milk. Drizzle the oil in slowly at the end while still blending.

Sunflower Seed Dressing

1 cup sunflower seeds
1 cup soy milk
1 teaspoon salt
1 teaspoon garlic powder
1 teaspoon onion powder
1/3 cup lemon juice
1/2 teaspoon turmeric
1 tablespoon parsley flakes

Blend sunflower seeds, soy milk, salt, garlic powder, onion powder, lemon juice, and turmeric. Stir in the parsley after blending.

Salad Dressing

1 cup olive oil
1/2 cup honey
1/2 cup lemon juice
1 tablespoon Italian seasoning
2 tablespoons onion granules
1 tablespoon garlic granules
2 teaspoon dill weed
2 teaspoon basil
1 tablespoon parsley
1 tablespoon salt

Blend oil, honey, lemon juice, Italian seasoning, onion, garlic, dill, basil, parsley, and salt together.

Sesame Seed Dressing

1 cup toasted sesame seeds
1/3 cup lemon juice
1 teaspoon salt
1 teaspoon onion powder
1 teaspoon garlic powder

Blend sesame seeds, lemon juice, salt, onion powder, and garlic together, adding orange juice as you go to reach the desired thickness.

Cucumber Dressing

1 whole cucumber with skin
1 teaspoon onion powder
2 cloves garlic
1/4 of a celery stalk
1/4 cup sunflower seeds
1/3 cup lime juice
1 teaspoon salt

Chop the cucumber up and blend it first. It will provide enough water to blend the onion powder, garlic, celery, sunflower seeds, lime juice, and salt until smooth.

Oil-free Dressing

1/3 cup toasted sesame seeds
2 tablespoons soy milk powder
1/2 teaspoon kelp powder
1/2 teaspoon oregano
salt to taste (approximately 1/4 tsp)
1/4 teaspoon cumin
1/4 teaspoon coriander
1/2 cup water

Blend sesame seeds, soy milk powder, kelp powder, oregano, salt, cumin, coriander, and water until creamy. You may add more water to get a thinner consistency.

Seasoned Bread Crumbs

3-4 slices bread
1 teaspoon sage
1 teaspoon thyme
1 teaspoon marjoram
1 teaspoon onion powder
1 teaspoon garlic powder
1/2 teaspoon turmeric

Place bread, sage, thyme, marjoram, onion powder, garlic powder, and turmeric in a blender, and grind until fine. Use as needed. Kindly note this does not have salt. You may add 1/2 teaspoon if you need to, but usually, whatever I am crumbing is salty enough.

Curry Powder

1 tablespoon turmeric
1 tablespoon cumin
1 teaspoon paprika
1 teaspoon coriander
1 teaspoon onion powder
1 teaspoon garlic powder
1/2 teaspoon fenugreek
1/4 teaspoon cardamom
1/4 teaspoon bay leaf
1/4 teaspoon thyme

Place turmeric, cumin, paprika, coriander, onion, garlic, fenugreek, cardamom, bay leaf, and thyme in a blender, and grind all together. Remove and store in a bottle. You can double or triple the ingredients to make to a large bottle. It keeps well.

Boulange or Eggplant Choka

4 large eggplants
10 peeled and sliced cloves of garlic
2 teaspoon cumin powder (geerah)
1 teaspoon salt
Pinch of cayenne pepper
2 tablespoons freshly chopped shallot or scallions
1 large minced tomato

Wash eggplants, but do not peel. Use a knife to slice into eggplant in different places deep enough to stick in your slices of garlic so they will not fall out. Now place eggplant to roast on a fire or a grill. This cannot be done in an oven. Roast it all around, by turning it by the stem, so that it becomes soft, kind of sizzled, and completely charred. Place it on a plate, and allow it to cool. Remove the charred skin and throw away. Mash the eggplant with its roasted garlic slices that should also be soft. When mashed, add cumin salt, cayenne, shallot, and tomato, and mix well. It's delicious with roti, crackers, rice, etc. If you choose to do it on your stovetop, cover around the area with foil, except for the burner, because this roasting can be messy.

Coconut Choka

1 coconut or 1 1/2 cup coconut flakes
1 teaspoon cumin
1/2 teaspoon coriander
2 grated garlic cloves or 1/2 teaspoon garlic powder
1 grated onion or 1/2 teaspoon onion powder
1/2 teaspoon salt

Grate 1 coconut. Toast the coconut on a low fire until lightly browned, and put aside. In a pan, place the cumin, coriander, garlic, onion, and salt, and cook, stirring constantly for 2 minutes. Turn off the heat, and add the toasted coconut. Mix well. Serve with rice or bread.

Tamarind Chutney

12–14 or 2 cups fresh tamarinds
2 cups water
1 medium onion, diced
2 scallions, diced
1 teaspoon salt
1 teaspoon sage
3–4 tablespoons honey
6 cloves garlic, crushed
5 chopped dates
1 tablespoon olive oil
2 1/2 cups water

Boil tamarind in 2 cups of water for 15 minutes. Let cool, and remove seeds. Add the onion, scallions, salt, sage, honey, garlic, dates, oil, and water. Cook for another ten minutes.

BUTTERS, CREAMS, DRESSINGS

Almond Milk

1 cup blanched almonds*
2 teaspoons honey
Pinch of salt
1 teaspoon vanilla
4 cups water

Blend almonds, honey, salt, vanilla, and water together until smooth, and strain through a sieve. Blanched almonds*—drop whole almonds into boiling water for a minute. Pour into a colander and rinse with cold water. Drain and pop off skins.

Soy Milk and Soybean Cheese

1. Use 1 pound of dry soybeans, wash beans and soak overnight. In the morning, rinse beans well.

2. If you are making milk, boil the beans for five minutes and throw off the water. You can repeat this five-minute boiling, as this step removes the bean taste from your milk. Repeat twice, or up to six times if beans cause you intestinal gas or bloating.

3. If you are planning to make only soy cheese, you can skip the boiling in step 2 above.

4. Place beans in a blender and liquefy using 3 cups of water for every 1 cup of beans.

5. Place all the liquefied soybean liquid in cheesecloth, and strain thoroughly. Squeeze out all of the milk.

6. The pulp remaining is called okara. Keep it because it is good to add to soups, and to make delicious okara cakes, etc.

7. If milk was your goal, place your milk in a pot, and boil it for 10 minutes. Watch it during this process, because soy milk tends to boil over.

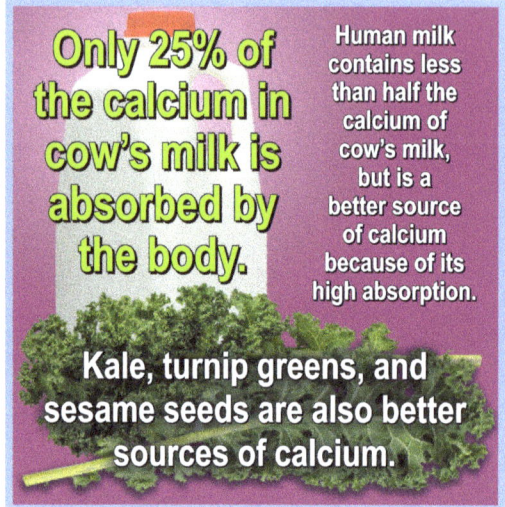

8. To every 4 cups of soy milk, add a pinch of salt, 1 tablespoon oil (do not use olive oil for this), 2 tablespoons honey, 1/2 teaspoon vanilla, and 1/2 teaspoon lecithin. Place in the blender and blend until smooth. It is very good.

9. For cheese, skip steps 7 and 8. Place 1 heaping tablespoon of Epsom salts to dissolve in 1/4 cup water, or get the juice of 1/4 cup of lime or lemon. Place your milk in a pot and bring it to a boil. When it boils, add either the Epsom salt water or the lime juice. Stir a little and turn off. Wait until cool. Strain through cheesecloth until curd is relatively dry.

10. If you want your tofu to form into a square shape, place the cheesecloth with the curds into the tofu box (a rectangular box with holes), and place a weight on top of it for about 5 hours. The curd will take the shape of the box. Place your rectangle curd under water in a dish and store in the refrigerator. It will keep for several days in this manner.

11. Now for the cheese, take your curd from step 9, place it in a bowl, and add 1/2 teaspoon turmeric, 1 tablespoon olive oil, 1/2 teaspoon cumin (geerah), 1 teaspoon salt, 1 teaspoon onion powder, and 1/2 teaspoon garlic powder. Use your hand to mix the seasoning well with the curds.

12. Press seasoned curd into a baking dish 2 inches thick. Bake at 350 degrees for 20 minutes, until the top is slightly brown at the edges, and there is a yellowing of the top. This cheese is sliceable, or you can crumble it. I enjoy it very much, especially when it is curdled with lime juice.

Soups and Salads

5 Bean Salad

1/2 cup cooked black beans
1/2 cup cooked navy beans
1/2 cup cooked garbanzo beans
1/2 cup cooked pink beans
1/2 cup cooked kidney beans
1/2 cup steamed broccoli
1/4 cup steamed carrots
1/4 cup diced sweet yellow pepper
1/2 cup chopped cabbage

Place black beans, navy beans, garbanzo beans, pink beans, kidney beans, broccoli, carrots, pepper, and cabbage in a bowl, and serve with a salad dressing or cheese sauce. This salad can be eaten as the main meal.

Bulgur Taco Salad

2 cups shredded romaine hearts
1 medium cucumber
2/3 cup halved cherry tomatoes
1/2 cup chopped celery
3/4 cup prepared bulgur
1/2 cup green olives
1/2 cup cubed avocados
1 medium onion, diced
2 tablespoons lime juice
1 tablespoon olive oil
1/4 teaspoon cayenne
1 teaspoon honey
Salt to taste
6 tablespoons salsa
6 tablespoons soy cheese
Baked non-GMO tortilla chips

Divide the romaine, cucumbers, tomatoes, celery, bulgur, olives, avocados, and onion into 2 equal parts and layer them in 2 bowls, beginning with the lettuce. Whisk together the lime, oil, cayenne, and honey. Pour over 2 bowls of salad evenly. Crumble soy cheese all over the two bowls. Top with salsa and chips.

Pasta Salad

2 ounces whole grain rotini, cooked and cooled
1/2 cup diced tomatoes
1/2 cup thinly sliced zucchini
1/4 cup finely chopped red onion
1/2 cup green bell pepper slices
2 tablespoons coarsely chopped black olives
1 teaspoon oregano
1/2 teaspoon basil
1 minced garlic clove
3 teaspoons lime juice
1 teaspoon flax oil
1/4 teaspoon salt
4 ounces white cheese

Place pasta, tomatoes, zucchini, onion, pepper, olives, oregano, basil, garlic, lime juice, flax oil, salt, and white cheese in a bowl and toss gently to combine everything well.

Cucumber Avocado Salad

1 medium cucumber, chopped
1 medium avocado, cubed
1 tablespoon lime juice
1 tablespoon olive oil
1 tablespoon marjoram
1/2 teaspoon salt
Pinch of turmeric
1/4 cup finely chopped pineapple or apple (optional)

Place cucumber, avocado, lime juice, oil, marjoram, salt, turmeric, and pineapple or apple in a bowl. Let marinate together 15 minutes, and serve.

Cabbage Quinoa Salad

1 cup cooked quinoa
1 cup raw cabbage
1/4 cup diced carrots
1/4 cup diced sweet yellow pepper
1/2 cup canned corn or green peas
1/4 cup sprouts
2 tablespoons fresh parsley

Mix quinoa, cabbage, carrots, pepper, corn or peas, sprouts, and parsley together and use with any salad dressing.

Normal Salad

1 whole lettuce (washed and in leaves)
1 carrot (shredded)
4 diced tomatoes
2 cucumbers (sliced)

Mix lettuce, carrot, tomatoes, and cucumbers together, and serve with a dressing.

Black Olive Salad

1 cucumber
1 red onion
1 can of black olives
1 cup of homemade soy cheese
1 large tomato
1/4 cup toasted sesame seeds

Slice the cucumber with the skin on. Slice onions into rings, slice olives into rings, and dice tomatoes into squares. Layer all on a plate, adding the cheese. Sprinkle the toasted sesame seeds as seen. It tastes as good as it looks. You can replace the homemade soy cheese with some seasoned tofu chunks.

Black-eyed Pea Salad

1 cup cooked black-eyed peas
1 cup chopped cucumber
1 cup chopped tomatoes
1 cup torn lettuce
1/4 cup finely chopped onions
1/4 cup scallions

Mix black-eyed peas, cucumber, tomatoes, lettuce, onions, and scallions together, and serve with sesame seed dressing.

Simple Tomato Soup

1 can (16 ounces) tomato chunks
1 can (16 ounces) tomato purée
1 can pimientos
Salt to taste
1 teaspoon garlic powder or 6 cloves grated
1 teaspoon onion powder or 1 onion grated
1 1/4 cup of water

Place tomato chunks, tomato purée, pimientos, salt, garlic, onion, and water in a pot. Boil 10 to 15 minutes. Enjoy.

Guyanese Soup

5 eddo leaves, chopped
1 cup calaloo (spinach) leaves
1 whole carrot, chopped
5 whole ochroes
2 eddoes (taro), chopped
1 sweet potato, chopped
8 dumplings
1/4 cup yellow split peas
1/4 cup whole barley
4 onions, chopped
2 heads of garlic
1 teaspoon turmeric
1 tablespoon salt
1 teaspoon thyme
1/4 cup whole wheat noodles (break them up)

Place eddo leaves, spinach leaves, carrot, ochroes, eddoes, sweet potato, split peas, barley, onions, garlic, turmeric, salt, and thyme in a pot with water to cover everything. Wait until the water is boiling before adding the pasta noodles. Boil until the ground vegetables are soft.

Broccoli Cheese Soup

1 1/4 cup cooked potatoes
1 1/2 cup cooked carrots
1 cooked onion
1 pound broccoli
1/2 cup cashews
3 1/4 cup water
1 teaspoon salt
1 teaspoon garlic powder
1 teaspoon parsley

Blend potatoes, carrots, onion, broccoli, cashews, water, salt, garlic, and parsley until smooth and creamy. You can boil for 5 minutes to heat through, or eat as it is.

Juices and Shakes

Juices are a marvelous way to optimize your nutrition, especially if you are on a busy schedule and don't always have time to prepare your foods. But even if you do have the time, juicing increases your nutrition and promotes vitality, energy, and disease prevention. Try to use sixteen ounces a day. Drink your juices fresh for maximum benefit. And your juicer will be worth the investment.

Green Drink Recipe

To make 6–8 ounces of green drink in a juicer, combine the following items:

1. First add a leafy green vegetable—such as romaine, leaf lettuce, spinach, etc. (or a combination of these) until you get about 1–2 ounces of green juice.

2. Next add a "meaty" green vegetable, such as zucchini, cucumber, or celery (or a small amount of all three) to give you another 2–3 ounces of juice.

3. Finally add some kind of fruit or fruit juice. Use variety. One day add fresh apples to the juicer. Another day add grapes. Another day pour pineapple juice into the above vegetable juice (or if available, add fresh pineapple) in the juicer.

Papaya Punch

4 cup coconut milk
3 cup diced ripe papaya
2 tablespoons honey
Pinch of cardamom
Pinch of star anise powder
Pinch of salt

Blend coconut milk, papaya, honey, cardamom, star anise, and salt. Chill and serve.

Carob No Chocolate Milkshake

2 bananas
4 cups milk
1 cup carob powder
1/2 teaspoon vanilla
Salt to taste
Honey to taste
2 tablespoons barley malt

Place bananas in the freezer for 1 hour. When frozen, blend with milk, carob powder, vanilla, salt, honey, and barley malt.

Watermelon Pineapple Juice

1 whole ripe pineapple
1 whole ripe watermelon

Cut fruit into pieces and pass them through a juicer. If you have a good juicer, you can pass your pineapple with the skin through it as well. Chill and enjoy. It is the author's favorite juice.

Cane Juice

2 cups pure cane juice
Pinch of ginger powder
2 teaspoons freshly squeezed lime or lemon juice

Mix cane juice, ginger, and lime or lemon juice together. Chill and enjoy. It is absolutely delightful!

Sour Sop Smoothie

4 cup sour sop without seed or skin
2 cup plant-based milk of your choice
1 teaspoon vanilla
1/4 teaspoon cardamom

Blend sour sop, milk, vanilla, and cardamom until smooth. Chill.

In Guyana, we make a lot of juice. We also drink a lot of sky juice also known as coconut water. When making juices, experiment with what fruits and vegetables you like. But by all means, drink some juice.

JUICES & SHAKES

Plant-based diets are gaining in popularity. People are seeing the health benefits of making grains, legumes, vegetables, nuts, and seeds the biggest part of their diet. Studies show that a plant-based diet fights chronic disease including obesity, heart disease, stroke, type-2 diabetes, and cancer. In fact, in a recent study from Ohio State University, children who ate fast food daily in the fifth grade, by the eighth grade were found to have test scores up to twenty percent less than those who did not eat fast food at all. *"Fast food consumption linked to lower test score grades in 8th graders"* (http://1ref.us/hi).

It seems that Daniel and his Hebrew friends in the Bible had it right. They were not only healthier but also brighter than the other students in the Babylonian school. See Daniel chapter 1 in the Bible. They followed the laws and reaped the benefits.

Rules of Nutrition: The **first** rule of nutrition is to be sure to include a **variety** of foods in the diet during the year. While variety is essential over time, the **second** rule of nutrition is that individual meals should be kept **simple**. The **third** rule of good nutrition requires that within each individual meal we eat **generously of fruits and vegetables, moderately of whole grains, and sparingly of nuts & seeds.**

Balance the individual meals keeping color, texture, flavor and variety in mind. Limit rich foods. Keep sugars to about three teaspoons daily, salt to a half teaspoon, and oil to two tablespoons. Avoid spices, greases, fried foods, baking powder and soda, and vinegar. Fruit juices and concentrated foods usually should be taken in moderate quantities. Eat your meals at the same time each day, and allow at least five hours from the end of one meal to the beginning of the next. The digestive functions are accurately timed and do the most efficient work when kept on a schedule.

Could it be that there are indeed laws of nutrition and lifestyle that determine health? I believe so. I believe, too, that many of us have food addictions that are harmful to our health. I believe we try to meet various needs with food, inner emotional struggles that we need to be healed from. But also, things that are fatty and sugary and caffeine-filled tend to be the things that we are addicted to, because those things appeal so strongly to our tastes, and to the dopamine or feel-good receptors of the brain. But while food should taste good, it should also be good, taken in the right quantities, and at the right times.

Kitchen Pharmacy

As a medical missionary as well as one who loves cooking, I could not fail to share with you some kitchen cabinet remedies. So here are some things that you use in cooking that works well in healing some common troubles. God's plan for us uses that which He has given us in nutrition and in life.

Pain and inflammation	Use the outer green skin of your cabbage and turmeric to make a poultice, and apply on the inflamed part, this will give relief.
Anemia	If you are suffering from a low blood count, consume raisins, prunes, annatto, molasses, and figs, as well as all green leafy vegetables, as these are high in iron.
Burning stomachs (Dyspepsia)	For burning in the stomach when eating, or more so after eating, try some cabbage juice or cucumber juice.
Itching	If you have an itch, try taking some oats and soaking them in some water for about an hour, then strain that water, and apply the water to the itching part.
Infections	Take 2 whole onions, 2 whole heads of garlic, and 1 whole grapefruit. Peel all and then chop up. Keep all the seeds of the grapefruit, place in 2 quarts of water, and boil for 20 minutes. Strain, and use a glassful every hour. This tastes horrible but does wonders.
Coughs	Place 1 cup of honey to 2 cups lime or lemon juice, with 1 garlic clove in the blender. Blend and take a spoonful every time you need to.

The Eight Laws of Health

1. PURE AIR
2. SUNLIGHT
3. ABSTEMIOUSNESS (AVOIDING HARMFUL THINGS)
4. REST
5. EXERCISE
6. PROPER DIET
7. USE OF WATER
8. TRUST IN GOD

About the Author

The author is Guyanese and works with the not-for-profit organization, Hidden Manna Ministries, Incorporated in Guyana, in South America. She is a medical missionary and has been working as a Lifestyle Educator for many years. As nutrition is so important to overall health, and because so many were calling for a vegan Caribbean cookbook, the author took on the project, and you have the finished product in your hands. The author conducts many cooking schools and lifestyle presentations. So if you are interested in us conducting a cooking school or health presentation, do contact us. In any case, the author encourages all to go to the ministry's website and take the free health quiz there for you. http://1ref.us/hj.

Guyana is the only English-speaking country on the continent of South America, which is also a part of the Caribbean. Guyana is bordered by Brazil, Venezuela, Suriname. Our closest Caribbean island in the Atlantic is Trinidad and Tobago. A land of six different races of people, Guyana is filled with food from African, Indian, Chinese, Amerindian, Portuguese, and mixed heritages. It is definitely a tropical land of culture and beauty.

Index

Symbols

5 Bean Salad 70

A

Ackee 43
Almond Milk 68
Amadama Bread 23

B

Baked Fries 34
Basic Bread Dough 22, 24
Basil Rice 40
Batter 64
Black-eyed Pea Salad 71
Black-eyed Peas Stew 41
Black Olive Salad 71
Broccoli Cheese Soup 72
Brownies 52
Bulgur 23, 25, 70
Bulgur Taco Salad 70
Burgers 38

C

Cabbage Quinoa Salad 71
Candied Pecans 56
Cane Juice 75
Caramel Popcorn 57
Carob Fudge Topping 53
Carob No Chocolate Bars 56
Carob No Cook Pudding 46
Carob Pudding 46
Cassava Pone 49
Cassava Puffs 42
Channa 43
Cheese Rolls 26
Coconut Buns 48
Coconut Choka 67
Coconut Ice Cream 47
Coconut Mango Ice Cream 48
Coconut Rolls 24
Colored Rice 34
Conkie 50
Cook-up 42
Corn Bread 23
Crackers 26
Cucumber Avocado Salad 71
Cucumber Dressing 65
Cucumber Relish 63
Cucumber Sour 63
Curry Katahar or Jackfruit or Potatoes 37
Curry Powder 66

D

Dahl 41
Date Butter 60
Dipping Sauce 60

E

Eggplant Choka 67
Eggplant Stew 34

F

Flax Millet Crackers 26
Flaxseed Crescents 27
Flaxseed Gel 27
Frosting 50, 51, 54
Frosting Cream 54
Fruit Cake 50
Fudge 53, 56, 57

G

Garbanzo Spread 62
Gluten Stuffed Bread 24
Gluten Tofu Loaf 33
Granola 16
Green Drink 74
Green Mango Sour 63
Guyanese Soup 72

I

Ice Cream 47, 48

K

Katahar or Jackfruit (baked) 37
Ketchup 63
Key Lime Pie 54

L

Lasagna 36

M

Mashed or Cubed Provision 37
Mashed Potatoes 42
Mayonnaise (eggless) 64
Meatballs 38, 39
Millet (Porridge) 17, 26, 51

N

Normal Salad 71

O

Oatmeal Patties 35
Oil-free Dressing 66
Olive Spread 62
Orange Cake or Muffins 47

P

Pancakes 16
Papaya Punch 74
Pasta Salad 70
Peanut Butter Cookies 55
Pine Tarts 25
Pinwheels 23
Pizza 25, 60
Pizza Sauce 60
Plantains (baked yellow and green) 19
Plantains (sweeter baked) 19
Potato Pie 36
Prepared Gluten 33
Pumpkin Pone 49

R

Raw Carrot Cake 54
Rice Custard Tarts 51

Roasted Eggplant Rolls 36
Roti 17, 28

S

Salad Dressing 65
Salsa 64
Scrambled Tofu 18
Sesame Seed Dressing 65
Sesame Sticks 26
Simple Tomato Soup 72
Sour Sop Smoothie 75
Spaghetti Sauce 61
Spicy Sweet and Sour Sauce 61
Spinach Quiche 38
Sugar Cake 49
Sunflower Seed Dressing 65
Sweet Loaf 46

T

Tamarind Chutney 67
Tennis Rolls 22
Tofu (scrambled) 12, 18, 33

U

Unleavened Bread 25

W

Watermelon Pineapple Juice 74
White Cheese 61

Y

Yellow Sweet Pepper Cheese Sauce 62

Z

Zucchini Cakes 11, 40

Notes

We invite you to view the complete
selection of titles we publish at:
www.TEACHServices.com

We encourage you to write us
with your thoughts about this,
or any other book we publish at:
info@TEACHServices.com

TEACH Services' titles may be purchased in
bulk quantities for educational, fund-raising,
business, or promotional use.
bulksales@TEACHServices.com

Finally, if you are interested in seeing
your own book in print, please contact us at:
publishing@TEACHServices.com

We are happy to review your manuscript at no charge.

www.ingramcontent.com/pod-product-compliance
Lightning Source LLC
Chambersburg PA
CBHW060941170426
43195CB00025B/2992